Joyful Journey
Listening to Immanuel

E. James Wilder
Anna Kang
John Loppnow
Sungshim Loppnow

Shepherd's House Inc.
P.O. Box 2376
East Peoria, IL 61611

www.lifemodelworks.org

A LIFE MODEL™ BOOK

Joyful Journey: Listening to Immanuel

By: E. James Wilder Ph.D.
  Anna Kang
  John Loppnow
  Sungshim Loppnow
Copyright 2015

ISBN 978-1-935629-17-7

Printed by:

Shepherd's House Inc.
P.O. Box 2376
East Peoria, IL 61611
www.lifemodelworks.org

Contents

Contents

Chapter One

Changed Lives

Immanuel journaling is a simple method for improving our awareness of God's presence in both our thoughts and lives. The method has three parts we will explain later:
1. Interactive gratitude
2. Writing our impressions – thought rhyming with God
3. Reading our journal aloud

There are many reasons to improve our awareness of God's active presence in our lives. The best reason is the guidance and friendship we receive from "checking in" with God throughout the day. Other benefits include healing emotional wounds, enhancing character and building community. This booklet will help you learn the Immanuel journaling method for use in your life and fellowship community. The principles involved will be explained using biblical truths for relating to God and neuroscience for improving our awareness. A more mindful attachment with God leads to clearer knowledge of who we can become.

"ME," my identity, is ultimately shaped by who I love and what pain I avoid. Love and the pain I avoid often compete within me to see whether my love or my fear of pain is stronger. As Christians we know "God is love" (1 John 4:8) and "Perfect love casts out fear" (1 John 4:18), but knowing this has little effect on our daily lives. Worrying whether someone will be angry with us often "casts out" our loving thoughts. What if we can show you how to interact with God in a way that is absolutely intimate and powerful and changes your life from the inside out? This process can be learned in a few minutes, and most people experience changes from the first time they practice it. Following a simple sequence naturally elicits transforming conversations with God.

Interacting with God is a simple idea yet it is something many of us don't know how to navigate. Most of us can neither see nor hear God, and we have some reservations about people who say they do! Even when Jesus came in the form of Immanuel (God with us), those closest to Him had difficulty seeing God in Him. Simon Peter, who went back to fishing, and the two disciples on the road to Emmaus failed to recognize Jesus after the resurrection (Luke 24). Jesus diagnosed them with *sluggish vision* (being *slow-of-heart*) as they were focused mainly on the pain in their lives.

We are like these disciples. We are *slow-of-heart* and have impaired vision of Jesus walking with us. Since we are all *slow-of-heart*, God has provided the Holy Spirit to empower us to experience Immanuel, the God who walks with us. Still, most of us can point to few, if any, conscious interactions we have had with God even though we somehow know that God is always present.

The Emmaus story highlights that God may be speaking to us and we do not know it. Let us examine three reasons why we might not be aware that God is speaking with us when thoughts go through our minds. First, our minds might not be in a *relational state*, one that is receptive to interaction with God or people. The relational state occurs because neural pathways in our brains have relational circuits (RCs) that may be open, alert or impaired. Like the disciples on the road to Emmaus, when we are in deep pain and our RCs are off, we also fail to recognize who is speaking to us. We will discuss this in more detail later and show you a simple way to reactivate your RCs and check whether they are working.

Second, we are told in Ephesians 2:10 to expect a similarity between *God-thoughts* and our thoughts. The structure in the brain called the cingulate cortex makes it possible for meaningful communication to occur between two different minds by establishing a mutual-mind state. When establishing a mutual-mind state, we learn to think and feel the way people we love think and feel. The interesting aspect of the mutual-mind state in the brain is that it works faster than the conscious mind so that we are never sure whether a mutual-mind thought is theirs or ours. We will show you how to develop a mutual-mind state with God later in this booklet. Now let's look at the passage from Ephesians in more depth before we consider the third reason we miss God speaking to our minds.

In Ephesians 2:10, Paul uses the Greek word *poiema*, which literally means God's poetry. When *poiema* is translated as "handiwork" or "workmanship" it misses the following important point. Poetry in scripture does not rhyme sounds; it follows the Hebrew pattern and rhymes thoughts. This means that as God's poetry, our thoughts can rhyme with our Heavenly Father's. That is amazing! How can it work? We know that as we become intimate with someone, we begin to finish each other's sentences and thoughts. In a deep, authentic, mutual-mind state, we actually don't know where our thoughts stop and the other person's thoughts begin. This is exactly what can happen between God and us too. A mutual-mind state with God results in an emulation of His character and heart; we are showing the world the poet behind the poetry. As our mutual-mind state becomes stronger, we are able to live out our purpose of being created for good works. It is important to note here that our "good works" do not save us. Good works flow from thinking like our Creator; we rhyme God's actions and not just His thoughts.

The third reason we miss God speaking to us is that we don't stop to check the characteristics of our thoughts to see if they are *poetry* that rhymes God's thoughts. We will explore how to check our thoughts more completely later, but now let us examine the main test. Thoughts that rhyme with God's produce *shalom*. Shalom is a state of harmony where everything works together, makes sense and is good. Shalom is the "peace of Christ." Furthermore, Colossians 3:15 tells us that we should let shalom act like a referee in our lives who "stops the action" every time shalom is missing. The Greek word *brabeuo* in this verse means to literally *sit as an umpire*, which suggests that this peace should be refereeing every aspect of our lives. The rule for our lives and relationships is that everything should be in shalom when we are synchronized with how God thinks. We will be in harmony with God and with everyone else who is making mind-poetry with God.

We lack the peace of Christ, shalom that referees our lives, because we have not learned to rhyme our thoughts with God's thoughts. Colossians 3:1-17 is a clear picture of what our lives should reflect when we are living and growing in a mutual-mind state with God. As we have been raised with Jesus and set our minds on the things above, our thoughts will naturally rhyme with God's through our growing intimacy with Him. As we put off our old nature through this intimacy, we clothe ourselves with who God is. In verses 12-14, we are told to put on compassion, kindness, humility, gentleness and patience. Moreover, we are to bear with one another, forgiving one another and ultimately clothing ourselves in love. This is the fruit of our mutual-mind state. With Immanuel's love guiding our lives, the peace of God rules in our hearts. We will show you a simple way to live in shalom.

At times when we fail to recognize the risen Christ who walks with us, our peace becomes shaky. We are not experiencing life as His poetry. Our thoughts do not rhyme with our Poet's and we lose *shalom*. When this happens, we should hear the referee's whistle blowing in our conscience reminding us that we are out of God's shalom. Immanuel journaling is a path back to shalom. Once shalom is restored we feel grateful. Gratitude and shalom are the hallmarks of thought-poetry with God so we have made them the beginning and ending points for Immanuel journaling.

Immanuel Journaling

Immanuel Journaling is a wonderful method we want to teach you to improve your awareness of God's mutual-mind state with you. Immanuel journaling was developed and brought into this teaching format by the authors of this booklet: Sungshim, Anna, John and Jim. Sungshim, Anna and John are pastors and leaders at their local churches. The three pastors met in graduate school while studying Marriage and Family Therapy. They thought like most therapists.

We were always searching for answers to help people and ourselves to be free from pain since we thought that getting rid of the pain was the way to live an abundant life. When we met Jim we were challenged and given a new paradigm. We realized we were going the wrong direction. Pain relief was at best temporary. Healing is not the absence of pain; rather it is a sound relationship with God and His people. Jim introduced us to the Immanuel lifestyle that taught us how to live with Jesus.

Sungshim adds:

At first I used the Immanuel Process for emotional healing as taught by Karl Lehman (Lehman, 2011) within my own church. In the beginning I focused on pain relief, but I desired to find a way for people to interact with Jesus easily and regularly. This led to our developing a broader tool called Immanuel journaling. Immanuel journaling not only alleviates pain but frees us from toiling in good religious activity that does not bring shalom. The Immanuel journaling process allows individuals and groups to become more aware of God's presence in their daily lives. We are excited to introduce a practical way to experience God's love and help that is easy to access even without a facilitator. We have noticed that even a one-time encounter with Jesus through Immanuel journaling can change someone's life. This life change has led people to share the goodness of Jesus just as the woman at the well did (John 4:28).

Immanuel journaling is the third system developed to introduce an Immanuel experience. Journaling has proven to be the easiest way to learn the process. Jim tested the ease of learning Immanuel journaling internationally with people from Argentina, Brazil, Chile, China, Colombia, Korea and other countries. Anna found Immanuel journaling worked better for her. John could teach groups at church and Sungshim discovered that people who learned Immanuel journaling could easily teach others how to do it as well. Not only were people growing shalom, developing in character and finding joy, they could also easily pass on to others what they had learned. Immanuel journaling is a method that can spread! In this booklet we have laid out the process for you.

What you will learn in this booklet

Chapter 2 introduces the term *iSight*. *i*Sight is having the recognition and awareness that God is good and that He is more than able and willing to help us. It outlines how we can strengthen our *i*Sight.

Chapter 3 focuses on *Interactive Gratitude*. We define interactive gratitude and why it is important to practice this discipline. There are examples that the readers can use to start their journey of practicing gratitude and listening for God's response.

Chapter 4 guides us through the factors that disconnect and reconnect us with our *i*Sight. Trauma and intense emotions can produce dimmed relational circuits in the brain. We can check our relational brain function and improve our connection to God and others.

Chapter 5 introduces the second step of Immanuel journaling called *thought rhyming*. We teach the sequence that helps find both emotional pain relief and peace. We list each step in the process and give specific examples of how they might be written. We describe a part of the brain that works in conjunction with each step and discuss the benefits of thought rhyming.

Chapter 6 discusses the final step of Immanuel journaling in community practice. We explain the significance of reading our journals aloud both in private and in a group. The skill of three-way bonding is strengthened when we practice this part of Immanuel journaling. We provide guidance for facilitating groups.

Chapter 7 is the Frequently Asked Questions section where we clarify some questions that might come up in Immanuel journaling.

How Immanuel Journaling changed our lives

Anna reflects on her experience with Immanuel journaling:

Growing up in a home where there was much pain and despair I had a difficult time trusting in the goodness of God and others around me. My life was marked by neglect, abuse, broken relationships, and my own bad choices that had taken a toll on my well-being – physically, emotionally and spiritually. I was a shell of a person by the time I had met Jesus at the age of twenty. My decision to follow Jesus was a radical change for me, and I was excited to leave my life of pain for all the promises that awaited me.

I was told that when I became a Christian, everything would be okay and that everything would be different. For me, this was one of the biggest lies I had ever encountered! Everything was different from what I was led to expect. Even though I had begun a relationship with a living God and the trajectory of my life changed to the opposite direction, at the same time nothing felt different. My family life and the people around me stayed the same including the deep pain I felt. Being in so much pain most of my life, I wanted relief quickly and when that didn't happen I became disillusioned. I believed that life would begin after I became whole. So I did everything I could to work on my issues and receive healing, thinking that I could really live my life reflecting the greatest commandment if only the pain was removed from my life. Obviously, I failed over and over.

God continued to meet me nevertheless. Through many loving people and resources, I, along with the authors of this book, have come to realize that healing is not the absence of pain; rather, it is the presence of God and His continuing involvement in our lives. Once this paradigm shift in my thinking began to sink into my heart, I began to notice that God was truly with me.

Immanuel journaling has been a significant tool in my life that has shown me this truth and has helped me to become more aware of God's presence in my life. When I was chasing healing, I found myself overwhelmed and discouraged; but when I began interacting with God through Immanuel journaling and with a trusted community of brothers and sisters, I began to live in the moment with God rather than waiting for healing to happen so I could begin my renewed life. One very practical element of journaling was that it allowed me to organize my thoughts and slow down the whole process of interacting with God. And because I was able to slow down and quiet myself, I was able to receive the precious gift of being able to experience God's compassion toward me. Once I started to receive His validation and comfort, I demanded it less from my husband and others in my community. I began to experience the joy of my salvation. As I built this foundation of interacting with God I began to be transformed in a very noticeable way. I now find myself becoming more and more aware of the shalom of Christ that also referees every aspect of my life.

Sungshim experiences Immanuel journaling:
I also began my transformation thinking it was a healing journey. My pain began in extreme poverty. I lacked sufficient food and housing and faced uncertainty about an education. Life could be a grueling burden on my small shoulders.

I am grateful that even during times of great lack my parents modeled faith in God. Their legacy was far from ideal, yet in times of great desperation my parents would cry out to a God who was bigger than they were. So, that is what I did. Deprivation led me to cling to God so I experienced His power and provision, especially when coming to school in America. As a result, my confidence in God's power to help the poor or the marginalized came easily.

There was an area of life in which I was not sure of God's power – His power to change me inside. My parents regularly attended Bible study, worship and prayer but God's power to change them at home seemed very minimal or temporal. As much as I promised myself not to live like my parents I found myself face-to-face with the stark reality of lacking the fruit of the Spirit. The failure of my faith to change my character became most evident right after John and I were married. Could God's power help me to love?

I began to notice Christians, like Anna, had a difficult time experiencing God's presence. However, Christians like me were seeking to love God by doing all the things the church encouraged them to do and yet, their lives did not bear the fruit of Spirit. Many Christians long to see God's power free them from addictions to mundane matters like snapping at kids and judgmental thoughts.

After searching and wrestling, I became aware that my capacity to metabolize pain in a life-giving way grows from an ongoing, interactive relationship with God and others. The active presence of Jesus showed me how to stay relationally connected to His Father in times of joy as well as during times of pain in a way my parents had not known. The love bond Jesus had with His Father nourished and strengthened Jesus to remember who He was, what He was to do and how He was to do it. In John 15, Jesus tells us to remain in God and that He will remain in us. He stresses that when we remain in Him we will bear fruit. Remaining is an ongoing interaction between us and Jesus.

One Monday when we (the four authors) were conversing, Jim shared that as a young man he was struck by three truths in the Bible he has tried to live by ever since:

- Talk to God about everything
- Do nothing out of fear
- Love others deeply

These truths struck a chord with all of us. If we practiced these three things, our lives would bear the fruit of the Spirit as a powerful witness to the world. Yet, our witness is weak because we do not talk to God about everything, we do things out of fear and we do not love others deeply. We have not become thought poetry with God. Immanuel journaling will help us "rhyme" our thoughts with God's thoughts.

Immanuel journaling is a tool that helps us to remain in Him. As we have shared Immanuel journaling one-on-one, in small groups and at conferences, we have seen the Father use this tool to help people live knowing that we are in Christ and Christ is in us—consciously growing in the awareness of God's presence. This gives us the capacity to love others because we know His love is continuously available. We can then take the energy we spent worrying and direct it to loving God, loving people and helping them know God. This becomes possible because we learn through experience that we are loved and will be taken care of by God. We will become people who can love others in the same way we are loved as long as we continue to stay in conversation with God.

We are excited that you will be able to experience the freedom we have experienced through awareness that God really does walk with us. We are encouraged that so many people desire an intimate life with God. We pray that you will find Immanuel journaling as transformative as we have.

Chapter Two

*i*Sight

Introduction

God created us as relational beings in His own image. Within the Trinity there is relationship and love is the "relational currency" of the Trinity. We thrive in life by interacting with God and His people in love. In story after story from the Bible, God reminds the patriarchs, prophets and people that He Himself would be with them and guide them. This truth is epitomized in the life of Jesus here on earth as incarnational reality. Jesus, Immanuel (God with us), was born as a baby to live His life with people on earth. Jesus shows us what it is like to live life with God. Bible scholars call this the "Immanuel principle of life."

We are confident most Christians would agree with the reality that *God is with us*. Abiding in Christ is a good way to live—actually the best way to live. The fruit we bear in our daily lives will testify whether we are abiding in Christ. Sometimes we fail to enjoy living in an Immanuel reality due to a distorted perception of God's character. God reveals to us that He is a good God through His Word and the life of Jesus. God is always glad to be with us. He treats our weaknesses tenderly. He actively works for our good. In other words, God is benevolently present with us. If our perception of God's character is distorted due to our own experiences of life's disappointments and our own histories of trauma, then having an all-seeing and always-present God could be stifling and produce fear instead of love and trust.

Immanuel sight (*i*Sight)

We become truly aware that God is good only when we experience that He is always glad to be with us. No matter what condition we are in, God welcomes our weaknesses tenderly showing us that He is always at work bringing goodness. To emphasize the importance of our awareness that He is relationally present with us, we will use the term, "Immanuel Sight" (*i*Sight). *iSight is having the recognition that God is present, is truly good and perseveres in doing good for us.*

Being created for relationships does not mean that each relational realm we are in is a safe haven for us. If our histories are full of people who loved and nurtured us, then it is likely that we experience easier connections with people and see them as our resources for comfort and help. But, if we have experienced a lot of pain or difficulties in our closest relationships, it usually shows up in the lack of close bonds we feel with people and ultimately with God. Some of us may find our *i*Sight weak or poor and being in need of correction for this very reason. This might help us to understand why many Christians maintain a life of survival instead of thriving. The abundant, thriving life with God is fully experienced when we have true *i*Sight.

We realize that some of us might become conscious of our poor *i*Sight and get discouraged by our condition. A word of encouragement would be that no matter where our *i*Sight may currently be, God can meet us there. Jesus spent three years of His life with His disciples. They saw many miracles and felt His unconditional love for them and even saw Him after His resurrection. Yet, it wasn't until Pentecost when the Holy Spirit came upon them that they felt confident in their risen Lord. This Spirit of Comfort (our Advocate who points us to Jesus) is here and for us, always strengthening the believers' *i*Sight. We believe that we are all called to come as we are. Whether we have distorted, weak or even no *i*Sight it is God who opens our eyes to recognize that He is good. God is here for us if we will just humbly open our lives to Him.

The good news is that we can develop, strengthen and even correct our *i*Sight through interactions with God. Discoveries within the scientific community are increasingly revealing that the human brain is designed to be in loving and reciprocal relationships. Humans thrive when we are connected to the people we love and who love us. If our painful past experiences make it challenging to trust in the goodness of God, positive interactions with Him will help rewire our brains to restore our *i*Sight. It is in loving connections with safe people that we become who we are designed to be. And now neurologists are even identifying that there is a region in our prefrontal cortex in charge of how we conduct ourselves that is nourished and developed best in this environment of loving relationships. Through these connections we actually become our true selves as God originally intended. We are able to have meaningful relationships and develop our brains and minds for success and abundance through loving connections.

Quality and quantity of interactions determine relationship strength

How do we define relationship? In Western culture the word "relationship" gets thrown around a lot. We esteem relationships and put a high value on "working at relationships." Although we have a general understanding of the word, perhaps the meaning has been lost. We sought a good working definition of the word "relationship." Two definitions stand out: 1) connection between persons by blood or marriage, and 2) the state of being connected.

We are related to people whom we call family because we are bound to them by blood or marriage but relationship speaks also of an ongoing, meaningful connection. This connection between people can be weak, strong or in-between. For example, Anna's relationship with her mom is a great illustration for this concept. She is related to her mom by blood and will always be connected to her because of this fact. However, the state of her relationship with her mom is very weak since she hasn't really spent much time with her, having been separated from her at age seven. The little time Anna has spent with her mother was filled with negative interactions. What contributed to Anna's weak connectedness with her mom? Two of the elements in this weak connection are 1) the lack of frequency in their interactions and 2) the negative quality of those interactions. If Anna and her mom had more frequent interactions of higher quality, then their connection could grow stronger. While these two elements would not be enough for Anna and her mother, they are central to improving our relationship with God.

Exercise

Imagine taking a ball of yarn, holding one end of the string while throwing it to someone. They catch the ball of yarn, hold their end and throw it back.

As the yarn goes back and forth you will notice that the connection between you becomes thicker and stronger. The loops of yarn provide a metaphor of how relationships grow through interactions.

The umbilical cord and the blood of Jesus Christ

The unborn child is nurtured and thrives in the womb of the mother through the umbilical cord. The child receives nourishment and oxygen through this vital cord attached to the mother and baby. Everything they both need is right there. Once a baby is out of the womb the umbilical cord is cut. How then do babies survive and thrive? Babies' needs are met through various interactions with their parents and others around them. Babies communicate their needs through crying and the caretakers do their best to feed, bathe, clothe, soothe, hold and nurture them in response.

Our relationship with God can be viewed in a similar way. Just as the belly buttons in the middle of our bodies remind us that we were once connected to the carrier of our life, the cross of Christ is a timeless reminder that when we enter into the family of God we are forever connected to Him through the shedding of His precious blood. As Christians we might all agree on this one point: the cross became personally meaningful to us because through the work on the cross we connect to God. Many Christians call this recognition and decision to follow Christ a "born again" experience. Just like a baby is born into a world, this is a one-time relational event. We must strengthen this connection by interacting with Him regularly and consistently. We, like an infant, need to be continually nurtured through interactions with God and His people in order to mature.

Many of us have heard of babies in orphanages dying because, although their physical needs were met, human touch and interactions were limited or absent. Of those who survived, many became mentally ill. Today there is abundant research that states infants cannot thrive or even survive unless there is a steady provision of loving interactions with parents or caregivers. God designed us to thrive by being in constant, loving interactions with Him and others.

Growing a relationship with God takes active intention and participation from each one of us. Imagine our ball of yarn metaphor at work in our relationship with God. When we appreciate Him we throw the yarn and when we cry out to God for help we do the same. As He responds tenderly and graciously He throws back the yarn, and the connection is strengthened. God frequently initiates these interactions with us. He beckons and waits for us to throw the yarn back to Him. Moreover, even when we are frail and cannot throw the yarn, His Spirit helps us. He never gives up on us and will work on our behalf until the end.

Is it our hard work or our interactions with God that bring about the response Jesus spoke of in the gospels?

Jesus answered, "The most important is, 'Hear, O Israel: The Lord our God, the Lord is one. And you shall love the Lord your God with all your heart and with all your soul and with all your mind and with all your strength.' The second is this: 'You shall love your neighbor as yourself.' There is no other commandment greater than these." Mark 12:29-31

The greatest commandment is to love God and others as ourselves. Moreover, we are called to be the salt and light of this world by obeying this great commandment. We know, however, that this cannot happen just by our will-power alone. That is why Jesus tells His disciples:

"I am the vine; you are the branches. If you remain in me and I in you, you will bear much fruit; apart from me you can do nothing. If you do not remain in me, you are like a branch that is thrown away and withers; such branches are picked up, thrown into the fire and burned. If you remain in me and my words remain in you, ask whatever you wish, and it will be done for you. This is to my Father's glory, that you bear much fruit, showing yourselves to be my disciples." John 15:5-8

The only way to live out our deeply held convictions is through growing an intimate connection to the Father through the Spirit. We believe passionately that *thought rhyming* with God is the only way we can fulfill His commandments and thrive. Is our current relationship with God, our connectedness with Him, empowering us to grow the fruit of the Spirit? Is the natural result of our interactions with God a life full of loving God and loving others? If our answer is no, then the Spirit invites us to invest our time and energy connecting our minds with God. This booklet is designed to provide two skills that can facilitate loving interactions between God and us and between us and others: 1) interactive gratitude, and 2) thought rhyming. Practicing these two skills will develop, strengthen and correct our *i*Sight.

Chapter Three

Interactive Gratitude

Introduction

We live in an age where we can be wired or "plugged in" 24/7. Wireless technology, though invisible, has infiltrated our lives and allows us to connect to the web and the cloud and venture into a virtual world with just the tap of a finger. To utilize the resources of the virtual world we need to log in with the correct username and password. In a similar way, there is an unseen and powerful spiritual world where we can connect with God, talk and relate with Him, and become immersed in His divine nature. Christians have access to the invisible but very real power of God's loving presence.

Gratitude: a password to Immanuel

Gratitude opens us up to the presence of God. Gratitude is a password into our awareness of the presence of God. We specifically chose gratitude because it is the easiest and fastest path to connection and because throughout scripture, God in His wisdom has always encouraged us to give thanks. **Immanuel means that God is always with us and desires to interact with us in all situations.** However, we often forget this truth or we are not really aware of it. Our awareness is often dimmed when we experience life's difficulties and become overwhelmed in spite of the reality of His presence and His desire to connect with us. We can become overwhelmed as the intensity of unpleasant emotions increases. The six big unpleasant emotions hard-wired into the brain are sadness, anger, fear, shame, hopeless despair and disgust. Feeling gratitude returns our minds to relationship with God in the presence of these unpleasant feelings and other forms of suffering.

When we are awash in emotions or pain, we naturally seek someone emotionally stronger to help us. While this would seem to be a good time to seek God, perceiving His presence can be very difficult when we are flooded with painful emotions. Interacting with God is only possible when we perceive His presence. Reviving our desire for relationship through practicing gratitude allows for easier and pleasant connections with God that motivate us to practice more often. When we keep practicing gratitude with God our brain remembers what our connection with Him was like making it easier for us to find our way back to Him even when we are experiencing one of the six big emotions. But connecting with Him by expressing gratitude is only where we begin, and Jesus welcomes all beginners.

Our brain is "plastic" in the sense that it is capable of changing throughout our lifetime. Whatever we do repeatedly tends to become a habit and increasingly easy to do over time. We are applying this truth very specifically to strengthening our connection with God. Eventually, it becomes a habit to look and notice that God is here with us.

There are other benefits to living a life of gratitude. From research in psychology, marriage, parenting and physical wellness, we find that gratitude enhances the well-being of our body, soul and relationships. The Bible urges us to live in a state of gratitude. Living a life of gratitude is something God encourages and even commands. We believe that gratitude is recognizing God as our gift-giver. Appreciating the beauty of nature or a baby's smile is appreciating God whether or not we recognize Him as the gift-giver. Gratitude is deepened by the recognition that I receive these gifts from God. Gratitude is recognition of our relationship.

I Thessalonians 5:18 says, "Give thanks in all circumstances; for this is God's will for you in Christ Jesus." All means all. In every circumstance we are told to give thanks. When we give thanks, gratitude becomes the vehicle through which we become aware of the presence of Immanuel, the God who is always with us. Gratitude in the middle of difficulties allows us to have *i*Sight. We encourage those who desire to strengthen their *i*Sight to start by practicing gratitude during times of joy rather than distress. Over time we can learn to enter into gratitude in times of distress, but it is easier to learn during times of joy.

The booklet, *Share Immanuel*, explains clearly why we should develop and how helpful it is for us to detect the presence of God's goodness in our pursuit of healing. Jim Wilder and Chris Coursey state in this booklet that our brains will carefully record the impact of trauma with intense emotional signals that will replay themselves in our brains intrusively. The impact of traumas throughout our lives combined with very few memories of being loved by God will create weakness. The authors state, "Nothing shows weakness as clearly as weak memories of God's presence combined with strong memories of trauma" (Wilder, 2010).

We tend to spend a lot of energy focusing on resolving traumas in the hope that we will be free from the pain trauma brings. What we often miss or overlook is the power of building memories of God's goodness that give us a sense of being loved. Noticing God's goodness and appreciating His gifts can be viewed as depositing money in our "Immanuel" savings accounts, whereas focusing on painful events in life can be like withdrawing money! Thus, the daily practice of recognizing God's goodness is always recommended to strengthen our brains to habitually notice Immanuel in every situation including pain. In other words, our *i*Sight will be strengthened as we engage in regular exercise of gratitude.

Interactive gratitude

Based upon the positive effect of gratitude in fostering connections in relationships we developed a skill called "interactive gratitude." There are two parts in interactive gratitude. First, we give thanks to God; second, we slow down to perceive how God responds to our gratitude. We will learn interactive gratitude by journaling. This interactive writing time allows us to build and strengthen *i*Sight. It is important to understand that the interaction between God and us is the defining difference between interactive gratitude and what we commonly consider as appreciation or giving thanks.

The response back from God is the essential part of interactive gratitude. Without reciprocity from Him we wouldn't be connected. As mentioned previously, two elements are needed in order to grow a bond between two persons: one is an increasing quality of the interactions and the other is an increasing frequency of these exchanges. This does not mean that we should avoid the six big unpleasant emotions in our interactions with God and others. In fact, it actually improves the bond if we have an attuned interaction with God or others while we are experiencing one of the six big unpleasant feelings. We will share how attuned interaction with God can be done in Chapter 4.

Many of us have been rightfully taught that prayer is conversation with God. Interactive gratitude is a form of prayer, thus it is also a conversation with God. This sounds simple. Why then do many of us only engage in a monologue with God and not a true conversation? We tell Him our thoughts but we don't listen for His response and miss the blessed opportunity for intimacy with Him. Intimacy with God is why it is so important for us to learn to listen for God's response. When we spend time in prayer, He will speak to us intimately about whatever situation we are facing at that specific time. Through His response we are assured of our place in relationship with Him. We develop trust in Him, and as we interact we become more and more aware of our place in His kingdom and heart. We need to hear His thoughts on our situation, the people involved and the details. Most of us pray so why then can't we listen? It's a skill most of us haven't mastered or even learned. It's hard to sit still when we are distracted or in pain. We are numb or we don't really want to hear because we are afraid of what we might hear. We are afraid because it is too hard to trust a God we don't see. In some traditions, it's easier to talk fast and loud which can alleviate some worry but for some of us that seems to be the only way we can interact with God. Talking without listening is an anxiety-ridden expression that can bring us some momentary relief but no shalom. God is definitely merciful and He does work through those types of prayer, but if that's all we have been doing, then we are missing out. We are missing God as the giver of peace in all situations. We are missing knowing that we are never alone. We are missing transformation. We are missing God's heart for us.

Practicing interactive gratitude is the easiest, fastest and even safest way of bringing positive changes to a powerless prayer life. Interactive gratitude also facilitates healing and restores our *i*Sight. Although at times God heals us instantaneously, most times healing happens as we practice loving interactions with God and His people.

John reflects on interactive gratitude

My morning routine on weekdays begins by dropping my kids at school.

As I drive to work I have a decision to make: do I jump right into the tasks of the day, get a boost by talking to someone at work or do I pause to interact with God? I want to know what will lead me to the most productive day, but each morning I wrestle with which path I should take. At times I look for someone to connect with before I start my tasks. This relational connection gives me some fuel for the day. However, this relational connection is not always available or helpful. Other times I start on my tasks immediately, thinking of how I can get the most done.

For the past few years I have developed a habit of prayerfully prioritizing my day with Jesus, which I call *My Daily Bread*. Before I begin prioritizing, I start with interactive gratitude. This daily choice to give thanks then pause and sense what Immanuel might be saying has transformed my days and therefore my life. Interacting with Jesus by giving thanks helps me start the day in a relational state of mind that connects me personally with the Creator of the universe. It begins my day with a friend who understands me, shares my mind and knows the things that make me grateful. We converse about what creates my gratitude as well as what we can do together today. The days I start by interacting with Jesus are more grounded, more relationally fruitful and productive. On days when I go straight into tasks I notice I am more prone to distractions. I am lured away by an article semi-related to my task or other "interesting" distractions. I drift away from my prioritized tasks. Starting the day with interactive gratitude has led me to better relationships and a more fruitful life. For this I am deeply grateful to my friend, Immanuel (Jesus).

Writing down our impressions of God's response

The first step in interactive gratitude is voicing our appreciation to God. The next step involves writing down our impression of what God is thinking and saying to us. There are many questions that arise for us when we attempt to write down our impressions of what God might be saying to us.

Some of the questions that arise are:

- How can we be sure that our impression of God's response to us is not just from our imagination or what we want to hear?
- Could these thoughts be lies from Satan?
- God only speaks through the Bible, doesn't He?

We may find writing God's response is difficult if we think we are putting words in God's mouth. We know we are capable of misunderstanding what God might be saying to us, yet the greater danger arises from never attempting or desiring to understand what God might be saying to us to guide us.

When we are thought rhyming with God we have the guardrails of God's character to keep our hearing on the right road. God's character is revealed by the person of Christ (the living word of God), the scriptures, the counsel of fellow believers, the presence of shalom and the fruit we bear.

One thing we would like to clarify is that when we write our impressions, we are not hearing and transcribing God's actual voice. In general, we enter a time of "thought rhyming/poetry" by creating a mutual-mind state with God. A mutual-mind state will shape our mind to see as God sees, but it can also reveal when our distorted poetry does not rhyme with God. We definitely do not want to limit the way God speaks to us, but for most of us (and most of the time) God's thoughts will arrive as an impression about His response to us.

It is important to note that when we write down our impressions of God's answers, we must later check our impressions against God's character. God's character can be seen in who God says He is in the Bible. The whole Bible reveals His character. Our thoughts of what God is saying to us need to rhyme with God's thoughts and His character revealed in scripture. We can test our impressions against God as love (1 Corinthians 13) and the fruit of the Spirit (Galatians 5:22-23) and attitudes found in the Sermon on the Mount (Matthew 5-7). If our impression of God's response to us is in alignment with God's character, it suggests that the source of our written impression is God. The peace and hope that come from this interaction are likely from God as well.

The difference between our imagination and a mutual-mind state would be that God's character would be misrepresented and not bring peace. There is room for error in our impressions of God. We are limited and our thinking is deformed. Let's have the freedom to admit that we can be wrong in our impressions of God, just as we can be wrong about our impressions of what our spouse or family members might be communicating to us. This fallibility does not stop us from seeking to understand what our loved ones are saying.

We cannot share all of ourselves or listen to everything God would share in one sitting. A vibrant relationship requires on-going interactions. Practically speaking, even in human relationships such as marriage, we have misunderstandings and must come back and ask clarifying questions. That is how relationships grow and work, even with God. God works with our ability to understand. Sometimes He allows us to have supernatural insight into situations, but often we become more attuned to God as we grow and mature.

If our relationship with our heavenly Father is a living one, we can speculate that we misunderstand Him part of the time, yet it should not stop us from continuing to have interactions with Him. What if we were to stop interacting or responding to our spouses for fear that we would not fully understand one another? Relationships are fluid, and we do not need to fear because God is good, and He will lead us.

Ultimately, if we are in an intimate and growing relationship with God, we will begin to exhibit mutual-mind states with Him. Our thoughts and His thoughts will flow fluidly between us and we will begin to think and look like the One we love. We will begin to like what He likes, love like He loves and grieve with Him for the things He grieves. We will begin to reflect Him more and more. Our interactions will mirror our growing bond with God.

We are loved by a loving and living God who desires to commune with us. God has promised His Holy Spirit to lead us to all truth and that when we seek Him with all of our hearts He will be found by us. We can trust and believe that God will reveal His loving truths to us.

Steps to Interactive Gratitude

Step 1) Gratitude from me to God

Take a moment right now and prayerfully ask the Spirit to help you remember a moment of gratitude. This memory can be anything that comes to your mind. It can be something simple that happened during the day or a theme you have encountered many times. When something comes to mind, take time to write down what you are thankful for in a conversational manner with God. Thank Him for those things (or events) that you appreciate. You may want to focus on appreciating Him for who He is, what He has done and how He has treated you. Allow the feeling of gratitude to fill you. If you are able, add why you are grateful for that particular experience. If it is difficult to remember anything, start your conversation by letting Him know your difficulty and asking Him to help you. Usually we find that when we are able to admit we are stuck it relieves the pressure of producing results. God meets us where we are and helps us to get unstuck.

Example

Dear God,

I am thankful that my friend Susan offered to help me by picking up my kids at school when she found out that I was at home sick. Her kindness reminds me of the truth that You are always looking out for me and finding ways to meet all my needs. You are so thoughtful and considerate.

I am thankful for Alicia who made homemade chicken soup and delivered it to my home. Because of her I did not need to worry about cooking, and our family enjoyed a healthy meal. All these friends' kindnesses led me to see how You are always working to bring goodness into my life.

I am thankful for my husband who dropped off the kids at school this morning. He did it in spite of his busy schedule, knowing that it would serve me greatly since I was not feeling well this morning. Thank you for his thoughtfulness and willingness to go an extra mile for me.

Step 2) God's response to our gratitude

Once you have written down your thanksgiving, pause for a moment to reflect on what you wrote. Next, ask God what He would say to you. Begin writing, but don't filter your thoughts at this time. Just start writing and allow the Spirit of God to lead you. Focus on putting down what you sense about His response to your gratitude. This is our humble attempt to hear God. What you write should resemble what good parents would say to their children after being touched by their children's gratitude.

Example

My dear child (or add your name here),

I am so glad that you were able to rest today. Even though your body was weak, you remembered that your spirit was lifted up through your good friends giving you comfort. I am glad that you recognized My love and care for you through Susan and Alicia. Thank you, too, for noticing My thoughtfulness and care for you. I am always looking out for you. I know you are concerned about your work. Remember! I am always looking out for you!

Once you are done with this part of the exercise you can either read it to a friend or group that you consider trustworthy and safe. Sharing our interactions with God is a blessing to others because it provides an opportunity to see God and ourselves in a fresh way. When we listen to one another's interaction with God, we get to interact with God, too. Through each other's stories we experience the Spirit that gratitude brings. Our brain actually amplifies joy as we share joy together.

Using Interactive Gratitude

On my own
In me - Enhancing *i*Sight as a spiritual discipline: We can begin to practice the spiritual discipline of giving thanks to God and keep a journal of interactive gratitude. The accumulated log of entries will help us see God's faithfulness, provision and goodness more clearly. This will enhance our *i*Sight and strengthen our brain to notice God's presence more naturally and readily in times of pain.

In marriage: Sharing interactive gratitude is a simple way to intentionally build up the positive interactions as a couple. This practice can strengthen the bond between the two and deepen their sense of being known by one another. A couple sharing in this practice can strengthen their bond, increase positive interactions and help each other to see the other through God's eyes.

In the family: Participating in interactive gratitude to God as a family is a great way to strengthen the family bond. This can become a family ritual and cultivate a culture of gratitude in each home. Here are some ways this can be done.

At mealtime: Families can include a time of gratitude around the family meal. To facilitate this, make a special jar (or box) together to collect notes about interactive gratitude moments written throughout the week. The family can read and reflect on these stories during a gratefulness meal.

At bedtime: John and Sungshim's family uses interactive gratitude as a bedtime routine. They begin with a simple song. "God is so good," for example, is easy for their young children. Then family members take turns expressing gratitude toward each other and Jesus. Some responses have included:

- I am thankful to dad for roughhousing with me when I wanted to play.
- I am thankful to mom for taking me to a soccer clinic.
- I am thankful to my brother for playing Legos with me.
- I am thankful to my sister for playing soccer with me.
- I am thankful to Jesus for calming my mom down when she was angry at us.

Once everyone is finished, they take time to quiet and listen to God speak, allowing God to share something He appreciates about each family member. Once listening is done, everyone takes a moment to share their impression of

God's gratitude. For example, Dad shares his impression of what God says, "John! I am thankful to you for roughhousing with the kids when you came home."

In my church

There are many creative ways to implement interactive gratitude in church groups. We have already had success with these methods.

1. Incorporate interactive gratitude as an opening part of gatherings in church. When we are in a state of gratitude, we can smoothly perceive God and others' good intentions toward us. Opening each meeting with a full awareness of God's good intentions helps us to become and stay relational while we are taking care of challenging issues.

2. Start a small group with the intention to grow *i*Sight. Each member could keep a log of interactive gratitude then share his or her entries with the group on a daily basis via email. Once a week they can meet in person and take turns reading their entries out loud. In Western societies, faith and relationship with God is usually very private and personal. However, God created His Church as a place that worships Him by expressing what He has done for us. This is a form of interactive gratitude. Stories of our interactions with God allow others to experience His joy.

3. Utilize interactive gratitude as a tool for pastoral care. When individuals come to pastors or leaders seeking God's wisdom, we can use this tool for equipping them to receive comfort and help from God directly. Receiving direct help from God allows people to mature in their faith and frees them from depending upon pastors or leaders at church. Church leaders and pastors can start the process by teaching interactive gratitude through practicing it together in person, through e-mail, by phone or even through written letters.

Chapter Four

Reconnecting

Living with unresolved pain
Many of us have felt utter frustration with dropped calls during an important conversation. The culprit is usually a bad connection or no signal. In the same way, we sometimes find ourselves in a crisis with a pressing need to call God for His help yet unable to get through to Him. We might believe God is there, but our relational connection is gone. As we mentioned in Chapter 1, the loss of relational connection is often caused by incompletely resolved pain. The mental activity of avoiding pain distracts us from relational connection with God and others. Being overwhelmed disconnects us.

Consequences of disconnection
If disconnection, like dropped calls, becomes a repeated experience with God, our trust in God begins to decline. We end up feeling abandoned in our

pain and begin questioning God's goodness toward us. Our distrust in God's goodness may grow deeper with repeated unsuccessful connections. Distrust becomes one of the roadblocks to *i*Sight with God, and we become stuck. Without interaction, many of us become hardened or indifferent to God altogether. After all, God seems indifferent to our suffering or incompetent or even cruel.

Without perceptible interactions with us, God does not seem present. Our living God appears to mirror the false gods the Psalmist describes, "They have mouths, but cannot speak, eyes, but cannot see. They have ears, but cannot hear, noses, but cannot smell. They have hands, but cannot feel, feet, but cannot walk, nor can they utter a sound with their throats." (Psalm 115:5-7).

Unfortunately, if we fail to connect to God many of us quit trying. Other well-meaning fellow believers may encourage us to pray harder or to study the Scriptures, but these remedies may also fail to restore our connection with God. We need to troubleshoot our "dropped calls." There is often a source of interference, and Immanuel journaling can help us find the cause.

Trauma

According to Wilder and colleagues, any life event that leads us to feeling alone without help can be experienced as traumatic. Whenever we perceive that God or people are absent during times of pain, or with us but unable to share the impact, this experience can become traumatic (Wilder, 2010). It is not the type or the intensity of pain alone that determines whether or not events will become traumatic. We require someone who shares our pain with us. If painful life experiences in the past were not consistently comforted, it will be difficult to feel we are not alone in the present. It will be challenging for us to sense God's benevolent presence. We often question and wonder if God has left us in our suffering. The Bible is clear when it says that God has never left us and will never leave us. He has promised that He would be with us always (Hebrews 13:5). In spite of knowing this, we can still feel abandoned due to lack of connection and our prior experiences.

Karl Lehman has extensively studied how our brains deal with pain (Lehman, 2011). Dr. Lehman states that experiences of pain need to go through a pain-processing pathway in our brains in order to fully metabolize and heal our wounds (Lehman, 2011). Pain-processing refers to the normal way painful emotions or experiences are fully resolved in our brains. Early in pain-processing we mentally ask ourselves if we are able to perceive that someone is glad to be with us during our time of suffering. If we believe we are alone and the pain exceeds our mental capacity, we become traumatized. We can get stuck at any point along the pathway; therefore, metabolizing pain is essential for healing.

Unresolved pain launches an automatic search for relief. Ed Khouri and colleagues explain what happens when we are unable to process distress and intense emotions then turn to temporary relief (Wilder, 2013). We seek behaviors, experiences, events, people and substances to numb our pain. Khouri explains how this practice usually becomes addictive. Addictions can then lead to even more trauma. The sad thing is that Christians are not exempt from this reality.

When pain has been fully processed, the experience usually produces wisdom. What caused us pain was not always a good thing, but a full resolution brings good from everything. This is redemption. If we allow God to take us through a proper pain-processing sequence, we develop deeper compassion and empathy. Moreover, those who courageously allow this process to bear fruit ultimately find they love God and others more deeply.

Suffering-well

Suffering well means that we go through difficulties in life without being traumatized and that we respond to each situation relationally. We were created as relational beings, but we forget that when reacting out of pain. In order to suffer well, we need maturity. All Christians are called to develop maturity. One of the main characteristics of a mature person is the ability to handle difficult emotions. Mature people are able to return to a state of calm from the six big emotions. Maturity rises to life's challenges rather than reacting from fear. Maturity allows us to live according to God's values, remembering that we are created in His image to do good works. Although life is not easy, we can still live by our values during challenging times.

Trauma hinders maturity and can blind us to who we really are. Many of us have experienced times when pain, rather than our Christian values, has determined how we act. When suffering well, we remain the same, living by God's values whether in pain or in joy. We have metabolized (digested appropriately) our pain and can remain integrated. Christians are to be known as a group of people who "suffer well." How transforming it would be if we all grew in spiritual and emotional maturity so that we handled pain in life-giving ways for everyone involved.

The life of Jesus on earth, which culminated on the cross, modeled suffering well. It was evident in the Garden of Gethsemane that Jesus did not want to go through with His imminent death. He was in so much distress that He was sweating blood, yet He was still able to remain connected to the

Father and think of the welfare of His disciples when the guards seized Him. Jesus did not change under pressure and exhibited the same thoughtfulness, forgiveness and compassion as before. His deep connection with the Father enabled Him to suffer well. God invites all of His followers to live our lives the same way as Christ.

Relational circuits

Our relational design is reflected in the loving interactions between God the Father, Son and Holy Spirit. As God is connected within this community of love, we are to be connected to people in a community of love. We are designed to desire connection and thrive when we participate in life-giving relationships with God and each other. Karl Lehman explains how God has actually designed specific circuits in our biological brains to serve our longing and need for relationship. Dr. Lehman has termed this part of the brain the Relational Circuits (RCs) (Lehman, 2011). The RCs are the part of the brain that helps us to recognize that we have a need to build relationships by connecting and interacting with God and with others. The central segment of the relational circuits is the same cingulate cortex system that creates mutual-mind states and thought poetry.

RCs are very much like our visual circuits. When we close our eyes, we cannot see anything. Or, think of RCs like a light switch. If we turn off the light switch in a room, we might not be able to see things as clearly as we did when the lights were on. When our RCs are "off," it is difficult to relate to others, including God. The obvious first step for interacting with God is to make sure our RCs are on. Our RCs allow us to perceive God's interest in us. When our RCs are "on," our natural desire is to connect and interact with people and God because we naturally want to participate in giving and receiving life and love and we value our relationships, whether we are in joy or in pain.

The activation of trauma-based feelings of being alone and in pain can turn off our RCs. The sudden blackout explains why we are sometimes unable to perceive Immanuel. God is always here to interact with us during times of pain, but our *i*Sight may be switched off. Karl Lehman uses an analogy of the ATM machine in relation to our RCs to help us understand this concept. When an ATM machine is out of order, we cannot access our own money in the bank. When our RCs are off, it becomes very difficult for us to access the memory bank of who Jesus (or anyone) has been to us. This metaphor helps us understand why we have a difficult time interacting with God when we are in pain even though Immanuel never leaves or stops wanting to interact with us. It is in our best interest to make sure that we are living our lives with our RCs on. With our brain operating correctly, we are able to experience God's involved presence and appreciate other people in our lives.

Dr. Lehman has created the Relational Circuits Checklist below that will help us to identify whether our RCs are on or off (Lehman, 2011).

Relational Circuits Checklist (Are our RCs on or off?)
1.   I just want to make a problem, person or feeling go away.
2.   I don't want to listen to what others feel or say.
3.   My mind is "locked onto" something upsetting.
4.   I don't want to be connected to _____. (Someone I usually like)
5.   I just want to get away, fight, or freeze. (versus Calm + Connect)
6.   I more aggressively interrogate, judge and fix others.

If we answered YES to any of the questions, then our relational circuits are OFF. Everything related to relational conflicts will turn out better when our relational circuits are back ON.

There is one simplified question we can ask ourselves that sums up the list above and assess whether our RCs are on or off. "Can I feel positive feelings about the person (or God) right now?" Being able to hold a positive feeling does not mean that we can state one positive quality about that person cognitively. We are checking to see if a genuine positive thought feels true in a way that opens us for interacting with that person or God. When our RCs are on, we are curious about what others think. We desire to connect and actively participate in building relationships. When our RCs are off we are unable to relate to God and others and see them as problems rather than emotional resources.

Many of us attempt to build relationships while our RCs are off. We do not realize soon enough that our RCs have switched off. This is partially due to the fact that RCs can turn off so quickly. We are usually not aware that our RCs are off, but others may say something like, "Something snapped," "He turned on me," "She went cold" or "He gave me that look." We have to deliberately work to notice when our RCs turn off. It is our responsibility to learn to notice.

Many Christians fail to recognize that turning our RCs back on is essential for restoring peace. In fact, it is our first priority. One of the first things to happen when we lose our peace is that our RCs turn off. We become focused on problems because we do not know it is possible to restore our RC functions. Our solution to solving problems with our RCs off is to do the right thing rather than restore relationships. Doing many right things with your RCs off can lead to doing very wrong things when it comes to restoring relationships in the Kingdom of God.

We can assume, from what Jesus said in Matthew 5:20, that the Pharisees were doing many of the right things. They might have also been right in the case of the woman caught in adultery (John 8), but they were unable to see the Savior right before their eyes.

Sungshim remembers:

I was one of those "Pharisees" who did many right things while my RCs were off. Interestingly, I was most focused on what a "good" Christian should do when my RCs were dim or off. Of course, I didn't know about my RCs then. I successfully served the local church as an associate pastor, was a missionary overseas, studied the Bible and attended prayer meetings regularly. Many "good things" Christians achieve do not require relationships, and success can be assessed by "right" behaviors. Looking back, I can see that is how I achieved my success.

After I got married, however, everything changed. My attempts to do many of the right things with my RCs off turned out very wrong and harmful for building a relationship with my husband. The harder I tried to fix my marriage, the deeper I fell into despair. During this time, I lived reactively, and I attributed my pain to God, blaming Him for not being there for me. When my RCs were off, I was not able to perceive Jesus as helpful and thus stopped interacting with Him. Even then, I still thought that I was including God in all that I was doing. However, I was living without the recognition that God was there to help me. To my surprise, my exclusion of Immanuel happened so subtly and unintentionally that I was not even aware of what was happening.

The quality of my life has changed from surviving to thriving once I humbly started the practice of keeping my RCs on and asking for God's help when my RCs turned off. The good news is that we can learn to identify when our RCs are off by beginning to recognize when we are missing the peace/shalom of God. Living in the peace of God every moment is a natural part of sharing life with God and doing His will.

How can we turn our RCs back on when we become aware that they are off? We offer interactive gratitude and thought rhyming as ways to restore RC function. Other options include doing the shalom my body exercises, practicing appreciation and finding validation from friends and/or God. Those interested in further exploration on restoring RCs can find help in Karl Lehman's book, *Outsmarting Yourself* (Lehman, 2011).

Chapter Five

Thought Rhyming

We are now ready to learn the second phase of Immanuel journaling we call "thought rhyming," based on the notion that we are God's poetry (Ephesians 2:10) as we discussed in Chapter 1. The steps for thought rhyming provide a structure with opportunities to slow down and receive God's validation in the midst of our struggles. When we experience God's comfort and help we become aware of His presence, and peace is restored to us. Immanuel journaling is designed to take us through the sequence our brain uses to metabolize pain. Following the order our brain uses provides the simplest path from pain to redemption as well as nourishment for our souls. Immanuel journaling leads us to a place of gratitude and where our RCs are restored and activated. In other words, Immanuel journaling is a tool that guides us through the pain processing pathway successfully. Ultimately, Immanuel journaling allows us to become aware of God's good, generous and tender presence in our lives, thus strengthening our *i*Sight.

There is one major difference between traditional journaling and Immanuel journaling. Generally, in journaling we describe our experiences to God in a *me speaking to God* approach. Prayer is also frequently about talking to God as He listens to us. However, Immanuel journaling expects that God not only listens to our prayers but also initiates conversations with us. God knows when we are unable to come to Him either because we are overwhelmed by our pain or because we are hiding from Him in fear. Just as He initiated the conversation with Adam and Eve when they were hiding, we believe that God approaches us, thus initiating our restoration because God is love. In Immanuel journaling, we thought rhyme as God describes our experiences to us. We write down what we perceive. Thought rhyming is a *God speaking to me* approach.

Even if we do not have positive feelings towards God when our RCs are off, by following the brain's recovery sequence while writing we can become aware of how God was making Himself known. We begin seeing Him as a good parent initiating conversation with us. The thought rhyming format allows God to start describing our experiences to us, and this helps us increase our awareness that God is with us even if our feelings say otherwise. The process of writing helps us perceive what He is saying to us.

Jim Wilder explains that there is a control center on the right side of the brain with four different levels (Wilder, 2004). This control center contains the systems Karl Lehman later named the relational circuits (RCs.) The control center is where we find the mutual-mind states that create "thought poetry." When Karl refers to the pain processing pathway, he is talking about the normal movement of experience through the control center and then out to the rest of the brain. The main function of the control center in our right brain is to handle emotions and social interactions. Handling emotions and social interactions maturely is what we have called "suffering well." The control center also contains our joyful identity that grows through relationship and practice in joy.

Perhaps we should name the parts and levels of the control center. Some people find that the names and explanations help them train more systematically. We will expand this explanation as we go along. Understanding the levels of the control center matters because the sequence the brain uses to grow itself is the same sequence Karl describes in the pain processing pathway, the sequence that produces mutual-mind states, the sequence that restores the RCs, the sequence used for Immanuel healing and the progression we use for Immanuel journaling.

Control center of the brain (right side)

Level	Function	Physical parts
One	Relational attachment	Thalamus + Basal Ganglion
Two	Personal reaction	Amygdala
Three	Relational synchronization	Cingulate Cortex
Four	Identity (individual and group)	Orbital Prefrontal Cortex

The sequence of Immanuel journaling

The sequence of Immanuel journaling is intended to improve our connection with God at each step of the process. Part of the Immanuel journaling sequence was inspired by the way a mutual-mind state restores our RC activity. Therapists call the process of entering into a mutual-mind state with someone "attunement," and the failure to reach synchronization is called "misattunement." In his book, *Outsmarting Yourself*, Karl Lehman emphasizes how receiving attunement helps restore our RC function. He explains that we will feel seen, heard, understood and cared for when successful attunement (a mutual-mind state) takes place. We no longer feel alone.

Immanuel journaling is based upon the conviction that God offers His children perfect attunement as a good parent does whenever relationship is needed. As mentioned in Chapter 3, if we experience God attuning to us while we feel any of six big unpleasant emotions, it increases our attachment with Him. Thought rhyming takes participants through five steps from God's perspective as God offers attunement to His children. In distress, God helps us restore our RCs and peace. Through the Immanuel journaling process, God brings healing to the broken interactions (misattunement) we experienced in life. Suppose we need to start our thought rhyming while we are feeling upset about something; we can use the following sequence.

1. I can see you
2. I can hear you
3. I can understand how hard this is for you
4. I am glad to be with you
5. I can do something about what you are going through

Step 1) I can see you

In Genesis 16, we find Hagar naming God after she was met by the angel of the Lord in the desert. It says in verse 13, she gave this name to the LORD who spoke to her: "You are the God who sees me," for she said, "I have now seen the One who sees me." Out of the many possible ways to capture God's character after her encounter, Hagar named God as the one who sees her and everything in her situation. It must have been very important for Hagar to be seen and noticed by someone bigger than she in this time of distress. She was a slave girl who could not survive without the protection and provision from her master and mistress. Here we find Hagar running away from her masters after being mistreated and left unprotected.

When our RCs are off because of distress, we find ourselves in Hagar's position, alone and hopeless. After the angel of the Lord met Hagar and she experienced being seen by God, she was able to return to Sarai. Her problem was not yet resolved. Being seen by God empowers us to suffer well in our painful situations without being overwhelmed. Our lives can be productive. The God who saw the pain and misery of the Israelites and Hagar is able to see the pain and challenges we go through today.

The way we respond to the question, "How does God see me?" is key to determining if we will move toward or away from God. In thought rhyming we write from God's perspective. God watches us with love and describes to us what He observes. To begin this for yourself, you will describe what is happening around you and inside you (as much as you are able) through the eyes of God.

There are ways that you can begin the thought rhyming process.

1. Begin writing about your observable actions and surroundings as if God is describing them back to you.

Examples are
   "I can see you sitting at the table."
   "I see you drinking a cup of coffee."
   "I can see you watching T.V."
   "I can see you staring at the computer screen."
   "I saw you pacing back and forth in the dark."
   "I have seen you yelling at your kids."

2. Write about your body movements, sensations, expressions or physiological responses that others might not be able to notice with their bare eyes.

Examples are
   "I can see that your jaws and fists are clenched."
   "I saw the heaviness in your chest making it difficult to breathe."
   "I can see your shoulders are scrunched up."
   "I see you holding your breath."

"I can see your heart beating fast."
"I see that you are about to explode."
"I can see your eyes tightening as tears are welling up."
"I saw your mind going blank and your body freezing up."
"I can see the knots in your stomach churning."

Synchronizing our brain with God
Step One

The "I can see you" step of thought rhyming engages Levels 1 and 2 of the brain's control center. Processing starts with attachment at Level 1 that moderates our bonds and makes all our life a personal experience. We carefully monitor whether or not we are securely attached to personally meaningful people. Additionally, the Level 1 brain initiates the emotional experience of joy when we perceive that someone is glad to be with us. The sequence of Immanuel journaling, a *God to me* approach, reassures our Level 1 brain that we are securely attached to God and that He is glad to be with us even if we are not feeling happy with Him. Level 1 is our first step toward awareness that God is here.

The Level 2 of the brain's control system is the amygdala, and it provides a basic evaluation of each experience. The amygdala evaluates whether we want to move closer or disconnect. All experiences are rated as good, bad or scary. If an experience is too scary, bad and overwhelming for us to handle, we disconnect or dissociate from that emotional experience. This means that painful experiences can get stuck in our Level 2 brain and remain hidden as traumatic memory. Instead of automatically disconnecting, what if we learned how to stay engaged with God? He has the capacity to be with us in times of fear and actively share each moment. Can you imagine how different life would be if we came to the place where we could confidently face all our troubles and trials without getting stuck because we are connected (attached) to our Father who shares this experience with us? That is what Jesus modeled for us over and over again.

Step 2) I can hear you

In the same story of Hagar (who named God as the one who sees) we discover another attribute of God through the naming of her son Ishmael. "You shall name him Ishmael, for the LORD has heard of your misery" (Genesis 16:11). We do not know what she has said, yet it is not difficult to imagine words of hopelessness and pain. Hagar is heard by God, who is bigger than her situation, her master and her mistress. The problems at home remain unresolved.

In Genesis chapter 21 we find Hagar wandering in the desert a second time. This time she has been banished. Her son Ishmael is now a lad. God again takes a great deal of interest in Hagar and Ishmael. He has heard her

---

Synchronizing our brain with God
Step Two

Level 3 of the brain is in the right hemisphere's cingulate cortex and creates mutual-mind states. As God hears us, God initiates a mutual-mind state with us (what therapists call attuning) to share His reality and let us know we are not alone. The cingulate determines whether we are going to create some mind poetry, based on whether we are feeling understood. When we are overwhelmed by negative emotions that are beyond our Level 3 capacity, we temporarily lose the relational connection to God and/or others in community and become non-relational. In other words, our RCs get turned off and we find ourselves feeling alone as if stranded on an island as the big six emotions overwhelm us. When God joins us on this island and shares our emotions, our Level 3 brain re-establishes relational connection to Him and others.

Engaging in steps 1 and 2 of thought rhyming during distress lets us walk through the valley of the shadow of death with our eyes and ears open and with God holding our hand to guide us. Our painful experiences go through the proper processing sequence in the brain. We live out Paul's words, "And we boast in the hope of the glory of God. Not only so, but we also glory in our sufferings, because we know that suffering produces perseverance; perseverance, character; and character, hope. And hope does not put us to shame, because God's love has been poured out into our heart through the Holy Spirit, who has been given to us" (Romans 5:2-5).

inner thoughts and initiates a conversation. God provides for their needs by opening Hagar's eyes to spot a well. God who heard the misery of Hagar and later the cry of the Israelites will not ignore our cries for help today. Now to answer, "How do I think God hears me?"

For the next step of thought rhyming we write what God is hearing us say out loud as well as what we are thinking internally. Listen as God describes back to you what He hears and write down His description. At this point we are just allowing God to describe and help us bring our thoughts to the surface, regardless of whether we judge them as good or bad. It may be challenging for us to believe that God can hear all our thoughts without condemning us. It is easy to get stuck because we start to judge our thoughts and ourselves. This step is focused on perceiving the fact that God hears all our thoughts. He is allowing us to experience being truly listened to instead of having us experience correction or teaching. In order to stay relationally connected, we must experience being heard.

When we slow down enough to pay attention to our thoughts, we will be surprised by the sheer number of thoughts that we have. Moreover, we might be tempted to skip writing down many of the thoughts popping up inside our minds since they may seem absurd or unimportant. It is easy to dismiss some of our thoughts because our left brain is trying to make sense of all of them. We want to get in the habit of writing down these thoughts that seem unusual or even irrelevant because sometimes these thoughts can be helpful in bringing to the surface something that needs resolution. In other words, there can be lies or vows embedded in these thoughts that were developed as a way of coping with our pain. When those thoughts remain hidden and are not replaced with truth, we retain pain.

1. **Begin writing as God simply says back to you what He hears from your speech and actions.**

Examples are
   "I can hear you yelling and screaming."
   "I heard you crying quietly."
   "I can hear you say to your child/spouse/co-worker/parents, 'I hate you.'"
   "Get away from me."
   "I do not trust you."
   "I feel unsure about this situation."
   "You do not know me."
   "I am done with you."

2. Continue writing about unspoken words in your mind. God simply recognizes what He hears from our inner thoughts. If there are too many thoughts, you can list them in bullet points.

Examples are
"I hear you judging yourself."
"I hear your heart and mind racing."
"I heard the excitement in your voice."
"I hear you saying, 'I am dumb. Here we go again!'"
"I have heard you trying to calm yourself."
"I hear you saying to yourself, 'I should be angry! It's not fair. She can't do this to me. I should have known. I wish I could have done it differently.'"
"I hear the deep desires of your heart."
"I am hearing your fears that you are too ashamed to acknowledge."
"I hear the quiet resolution in your heart."

Step 3) I can understand how big (hard) this for you

In the story of Hagar, we may empathize with her pain, knowing her marginalized status as a foreigner and the abandonment she may have felt. The unfair treatment from Sarai may arouse our compassion for Hagar as the victim, or we might think that Hagar deserved this treatment for her sin of despising her mistress. We may feel sorry for Sarai or even Abram. We also minimize our pain. Often we deny ourselves permission to receive comfort for the seemingly small moments of pain. We minimize our apparently minor trials, compared to the perceived bigger challenges of others. We do this to ourselves and to others. God, however, sees, hears, knows and understands why a particular issue is so big for us. God knows our history. No matter how insightful a therapist may be or wise a friend is, only God can ultimately know the intricacies of our lives and experiences. His eyes never leave us, and He knows us better than we know ourselves.

Validation moves mental experiences toward resolution by accurately stating their "size," that is to say, intensity and impact. Without validation we will not be comforted. Comfort follows validation and gives us peace. When we validate how big or hard our experiences were, we can then calm our brain.

In this third step, we put in words our impression of God's accurate understanding of how important something is to us. He is able to illuminate our responses and grant us forgiveness, understanding, and comfort. He also gives us a model to follow. Through this step we may discover we are reacting to something in the past.

Synchronizing our brain with God
Step Three

Step 3 of thought rhyming engages the fourth (top) level of the brain's control center. Here we accumulate all the wisdom we have gained from sharing mutual-mind states with greater minds than ours who love us (Level 1) and maintain a relationship with us (they suffer well at Level 3) even when we hurt. Our accumulated wisdom shows us how to act like our true selves and stay relational during every part of life. The first part of a healthy Level 4 response is to validate how intense our reaction actually is. Securely attached children begin validating themselves as early as 18 months of age. When we have suffered many misattunements (poor or no mutual-mind) we tend to invalidate, accuse and blame instead of validating. This is a malfunction of Level 4.

During moments of thought rhyming with God, His validation of how big something feels also becomes our validation. We can share validation because our mutual-mind with God was established in the previous step. Validation requires accuracy about the size of our reaction and not agreement about the cause. We must always validate the actual size of our reactions and not try to resize our emotions into what we wish they were. Validation "gets" the size right. Now the executive control center can take over and handle this event relationally in the way that rhymes with how God sees me.

The Level 4 brain (which is the right-sided orbital prefrontal cortex (PFC)) has executive control over the rest of the brain when properly developed. The PFC is our captain. The PFC thinks of itself as "me" and takes ownership of our identity. When trained, the PFC captain has the capacity to quiet our reactions, direct our moral choices, be creative, think flexibly and even influence such delicate functions as our immune system. When the captain is strong enough, and the three levels below it have sufficient capacity, the mind can resist becoming traumatized. Even when things are difficult, the mature PFC captain maintains a strong, positive and determined identity. Level 4 discerns how we can navigate a situation to a satisfying resolution. With the PFC captain in charge, even negative emotions become calm and peaceful.

Examples

"I can see this is a pretty big deal for you."

"This feels all-consuming for you."

"It looks like this is about to overtake you."

"This is as big as when your parents announced their divorce."

"This is a big deal, but workable."

"I understand how sad you feel about this."

"I understand how angry you are; it makes sense to me."

"I understand why this is so hard for you. You have always felt alone so even though you understand in your head, your heart is about to burst with fear."

"I understand why this is so big and scary for you. I know you feel like you are not able to get My attention, and that scares you. I know that growing up, you or your experiences were never the priority for your parents."

Step 4) I am glad to be with you and treat your weaknesses tenderly

The angel of the Lord found Hagar in the desert. Hagar was running away from her mistress, Sarai, who was not glad to be with her and who had treated her harshly. The angel approached Hagar showing initiative, which we see mirrored when Jesus initiated conversation with the woman at the well. While no one wanted to interact with these women and treated them with contempt, God engaged them in love and treated their weaknesses tenderly. Hagar and Ishmael's sin toward Sarai and Isaac drew hatred and contempt from Sarai, yet did not push God away.

We think that our sin or weaknesses will keep God away from us. We might even think God cannot associate with sinners. However, God is always glad to be with us just as we are. Whether we feel connected to God or not, none of our weaknesses keep Him away. In God's presence we are transformed.

In step 4 you will write God's confirmation of His love for you by hearing Him say, "I am glad to be with you, my child." Write what you perceive God might be saying to you in a kind, tender and loving way.

Examples

"I am glad to be with you. And I see your weakness tenderly."

"I am always glad to interact with you anytime including this moment of frustration/pain/sadness. You might judge and condemn your lack of trust in My goodness and love but I never condemn you. Rather, I am glad and thankful that you are here with Me."

We let God help us return to joy in steps 3 and 4 of thought rhyming. The way that Jesus helped Peter is a good illustration. Jesus seemed to know how big it was for Peter to have denied Him three times (John 21). Peter felt defeated and hopelessly retreated back to fishing even after He knew of Jesus' resurrection. Jesus found Peter and invited him back three times in parallel to Peter's three denials. Peter was restored once he experienced that Jesus still wanted him in spite of his weakness. Once we return to joy with God's help we can live as His children.

Step 5) I can do something about what you are going through

Let us take a look at Hagar's story again. The angel of the Lord showed Hagar God's active goodness in her life. God gave her a name for her son and the promised hope of many descendants. The angel also told Hagar (who was running away) to return to her life as a slave. This meant doing something difficult. God not only validates our pain, but also guides us in our difficult situations.

In step 5 of thought rhyming, we write down what God might be saying to us about how He will be with us and help us. We may be reminded of God's faithfulness in the past and given hope of His continuing work in, around and through us. Scripture quotes and stories often come to mind during this time. Sometimes we find God asking us to do the difficult and hard work of living as His children. While reminding us who we are, God invites us to live according to our true heart. The promise of His constant presence, His unfailing love and His pure goodness will sustain us. Write your impression of what God is offering you.

Examples

"I will help you. I will help you to continue to see more clearly who I am and what I have been doing in your life and in this world. I will continue to make your heart tender so that the seeds of My Word and My Spirit will be able to grow and thrive in your life. I have you in the palm of My hands. I love you."

"My Spirit will hold you. We are praying for you. We are upholding you. We are protecting you. We are shielding you and always encouraging you. Look up, My child, in your despair and see through the eyes of heaven. We will never let you go, and we will never let you stay down. We love you intensely and without borders. Our love for you is greater than your inability to trust and your idolatry and your fear. We will get through this. We are protecting your children. We are your God, the Father, the Son and the Holy Spirit. We are powerful and beyond measure."

"I will uphold you with My righteous right hand. Meditate on My goodness and on My truth. You will begin to see clearly, and the spirit of confusion and self-condemnation will leave. I will be with you tonight and give you good rest. I want you to sleep knowing that we can resolve this together. I will give you the words to speak to clarify the situation, and I will give you a heart of flesh so that you may be able to see from her perspective."

These five steps form the sequence of thought rhyming with God. His perfect attunement and validation reveal to us that He truly sees. God is glad to be with us in all circumstances. He is always initiating the restoration of our relationships with Him and others. He is continuously working on our behalf. Immanuel journaling allows us to be more aware of these truths.

Using Immanuel Journaling with thought rhyming

On my own
Immanuel journaling is designed for restoring peace and joy. It can be used as a tool to facilitate personal healing and maturity in many different ways.

Turning my RCs back on: Once we recognize that our RCs are off, we can engage in the Immanuel journaling process to restore God's peace and joy. Many of us do not know how to process our mistakes and failures with God, and that is why we tend to get stuck in our pain. We can review our painful events or memory in a safe way through Immanuel journaling, and it can give us wisdom and compassion for ourselves and others.

Facilitating my healing and growing in maturity: Traumas, in general, contain the memory of pain without a memory of God's presence (Lehman, 2011). These traumas become blockages to our own maturity. Immanuel journaling can be used as a tool to facilitate the process of healing. The recognition of God's presence in each traumatic memory makes it no longer traumatic, but healing and hopeful.

Personal spiritual discipline: Spiritual maturity grows when we develop the habit of creating space where we can reflect on our lives. Regularly practicing Immanuel journaling is asking one simple question, "Jesus, is there anything

You want me to know about this situation?" As we attempt to listen, we are increasing our awareness of God's presence as His peace guides our lives.

In marriage: Immanuel journaling helps all relationships, and especially intimate connections in our lives. If we are married or have children, we understand that the daily grind of tasks versus nurturing relationships is hard to balance. An unbalanced life takes a toll on our work performance, health, children, academic pursuits and family. When conflict develops, we are usually directed to work on communication. We attempt to restore our peace using communication skills. How effective is that? When we turn to others, hoping that communicating will restore our peace, the road can be a little rough. When we use Immanuel journaling with God to restore our peace before we communicate with others, it can give us strength and wisdom. Many misunderstandings can benefit from slowing down and talking to God about our own fears and triggers. Once we have shalom inside, the referee of God's Spirit (Colossians 3:15) allows us to return to talking with others. Now we are sharing our peace instead of searching for it.

In parenting: Parenting can be a great source of joy or anxiety. There may be circumstances that require more patience and kindness than we can muster at the moment. We want to share how to utilize Immanuel journaling as a way of strengthening our relationship with our children.

    a. **Providing attunement to our children to help restore their RCs:** When our children's RCs are off it is the parents' job to help restore their RCs. We, the adults, are supposed to have better developed brains. However, many of us are in the process of rewiring our own poorly trained brains. In the middle of a conflict, where distress is being amplified, it is really difficult to help the child, let alone restore our own RCs. Consider using the Immanuel journaling's sequence, verbally if necessary, as a tangible way to help restore our own RCs while helping our children's RCs. The Immanuel sequence helps calm both parents and children. Many times children are fighting their own big feelings, and we all need to experience God's attunement and shalom.

    b. **Repairing misattunement with our children by sharing our interaction with God:** Attachment research tells us the importance of repair after we fail to connect with our children in their time of need. When we react to our children in our out of control moments, we may spend a lot of energy whipping ourselves. We know very well that we failed to live out our commitment to parenting. We cannot avoid failures in parenting, but we can work toward rapid repairs. We recommend using Immanuel journaling as a way of restoring your own peace as the first step. Once you are well connected with God, you can tell your children how God interacted with you. If your children are young, we suggest summarizing your impression of God's thoughts to you as a parent, rather than reading the whole entry. However, if your children are old enough, we suggest reading your interaction with God. This teaches and models that we all have access to God in times of need.

In my church

Immanuel journaling can be used as a tool/homework for individuals who are receiving care from pastors and spiritual directors. Church leaders can introduce Immanuel journaling as a pain processing tool for hurting individuals. Many pastors and small group leaders face an endless stream of people in pain who want to talk about their problems. Some people, in particular, call someone whenever they need validation or comfort. Once the validation wears off they go back or find someone else to listen to them. Their vast need for validation soon results in others avoiding them or pushing them away. Immanuel journaling equips people with skills to interact with God for validation, comfort and lasting peace.

Immanuel journaling can be used in small groups to facilitate a closer connection with God. Gathering on a regular basis as a group and using the time to practice Immanuel journaling is a rapid way to see transformation in participants. After writing one's Immanuel journaling entry, each person is encouraged to read it aloud. When Immanuel journaling is practiced in a group setting, we notice many added benefits for participants, such as the amplification of joy and peace. Participants benefit from reading their own entry as well as listening to others. We will explore the benefits of practicing Immanuel journaling as a community in Chapter 6.

Another way of facilitating an Immanuel journaling group is doing Immanuel journaling individually and sharing it via email before meeting. Participants bring a significant entry when meeting as a group and read it aloud. We will now examine the many ways that sharing our thought rhyming with God helps build character, fellowship, shalom and maturity.

Chapter Six

Creating an Immanuel Community

John tells us:

I remember in the beginning of my college years, I yearned for a way to communicate with Jesus as if He was physically present. I wanted to share in that communication with my friends. I remember saying to my friends, "Why can't we talk as if Jesus were with us, and hear from Him?" My friends just sort of nodded and didn't know what to say or do, so we moved on. Because I didn't have any way of concretely doing that, I was stuck – until now. Practicing Immanuel journaling in a group has been one concrete way I've experienced the joys of sharing life in Christ. The hour to hour and a half of engaging in Immanuel journaling together has brought me a depth of joy and shared life in Christ that has rarely been matched anywhere else. I am thankful that a group of us gather together practicing this on a weekly basis (when kids were in school) to deepen our life in Christ. I hope that others open up their hearts and schedules to practice Immanuel journaling in a group to experience this new depth of life. Sharing time, slowing down and checking for shalom can bring the body of Christ together in a meaningful and creative way.

Reading our Immanuel journal aloud

The final step of reading our Immanuel journaling aloud brings harmony deep within our hearts, minds and souls. Reading aloud is a simple step that takes our experience to another level. Some people might be tempted to skip this step since their interaction with God in writing brought so much relief that they feel better. Nevertheless, when people read aloud their interaction with God, an integrative and a restorative experience takes place. Reading aloud can take what was experienced alone into the presence of love and compassion from others. When we read aloud, we blend the words of the left brain with the emotional experience of the right brain. Therefore, reading aloud has benefits for us internally and externally. The community also becomes a chorus that amplifies all the good outcomes of the Immanuel journaling experience. As things begin to fit together, we feel shalom that is amplified as we speak and others listen.

The reader

When we take time to read our Immanuel journaling entries to trusted people, it allows us to hear for ourselves the conversation we had with God. We overcome shame about our weaknesses by reading aloud in community how God sees us. Others can amplify the joy and peace our time with God produced in us. In this way, we are sharing the love that we have received from God. Our conversations become rich and real. As we hear ourselves read the words, they become tangible expressions of God's care and goodness towards us. God's thoughts do not just stay in our heads or in our notebooks, but become living experiences in our heart. Our hearers are also blessed. Like the woman at the well who encountered Jesus, when we meet God face to face we cannot help but run to tell everyone. The woman at the well was amazed that Jesus knew her better than she knew herself and went to tell everybody in her village about Him. She overcame her shame about her life while sharing about a God who was good, kind and loving. Her joy and hope brought the whole village back to taste what she had experienced. It is our responsibility and privilege to tell others about our gratitude for God's power in our lives. When our conversations center on who God is and His effects on us, the church becomes attractive enough to draw the world to God.

The listener

When we are listening to others read their interactions with God, we are offering them joy. The Bible clearly speaks of the wisdom in listening. By listening without interrupting, we participate in God's work by creating a sacred space for people to encounter themselves, their community and God. In this space God provides perfect attunement. As we listen to them, we become a tangible sign of God's attunement. Our listening strengthens our community. We rejoice with those who rejoice, and weep with those who weep (Romans 12:15). We celebrate with those who are growing, conversing with God and discovering practical ways to live the gospel. We can weep with those who are grieving, hurting, aching, and struggling to stay on their journey with God.

Listening requires hospitality and generosity. Taking time to walk with our community stretches us because sometimes it is inconvenient and painful. It can be hard to listen when our own wounded areas are stimulated by another's experience. Yet even painful shared moments can be healing for us. As our brothers and sisters hear from God and experience shalom, our trust that God is good will also grow. Trust grows our bond with God and roots us deeply in a community identity based on Immanuel shalom.

There is one other listener each time we read our Immanuel journaling aloud - our own brain. The brain processes thinking and listening somewhat differently. When we read our own writing aloud, the words and meanings go to new places, and we often surprise ourselves with the deeper meaning achieved as we read aloud.

Taking a step of faith

Reading our intimate interaction with God to a friend or in front of small group can be a difficult thing for some of us. We are aware that there might be resistance within us. Some of us might be concerned that our story is not significant or important enough for others' time and attention. We might be afraid that listeners might judge, misunderstand or even reject us. There is an element of risk involved in sharing our most intimate thoughts and feelings with others, especially if we have experienced being hurt when we have been vulnerable. People may have despised, rejected, punished or even taken advantage of our weaknesses.

The number one ground rule when sharing our entries is to treat every weakness tenderly. As individuals or a group, we show maturity by treating our own weaknesses and those of others with compassion. This is not a 100% risk-free experience because we must learn compassion for the stormy waves of our lives and emotions. If you want to walk on water, we encourage you to step outside the boat and grab Jesus by the hand. Like Peter, when we start to sink we look back to Jesus and share the peace in His eyes.

Sharing our Immanuel journaling entry with others amplifies the effects

It is time to examine the benefits of Immanuel journaling that go beyond being an individual experience. The benefits of sharing the experiences that bring us peace, as Immanuel journaling does, are profound for both the reader and listener. Let us examine the top three.

1. Sharing our Immanuel journaling entry can amplify joy and peace in us and in others who listen to our entry.
2. Sharing our Immanuel journaling entry can help us to form three-way family bonds and develop a group identity as God's children.
3. Sharing our Immanuel journaling entry can help us to integrate misplaced or misunderstood parts of our story into a coherent and redemptive life story.

Amplifying joy and peace

Our most powerful communication does not come from our words because our brains are designed to pick up signals of other's moods and feelings through facial expressions, voice tone, posture, timing and other body language. The brain is a natural amplifier for these feeling signals. When two people are sharing the same feelings those feelings are intensified. If one brain shares another's joy, the result is amplified joy for both brains. This is also true for distress.

In a world full of distress, natural disasters, crimes against women and children and so much more, our brains could spend the day amplifying distress. However, as Christians we are to live differently. Our lives should shine with hope, joy, peace, and love. How can we do this in a world that is saturated with struggles and pain? To create a new culture of joy and peace in a practical way, we must find and amplify joy. We amplify the news of hope when we share and listen to Immanuel stories of how God has returned us to joy from our distress and restored us to shalom in God's presence.

Forming three-way bonds and a group identity as God's people

Our culture glorifies two-way bonds in romantic relationships or as two best friends. We do not do so well with three or more people at a time. "Two is company, but three is a crowd," we say. While mutual-mind states can only be shared by two people at a time, our group identity requires three or more people to share an identity. The Life Model calls this family way of bonding a three-way bond. This challenging skill is crucial to building community. An example of a three-way bond (family bond) is the way mother enjoys watching father delight in their baby. Father also enjoys watching mother and child bond the same way. If the father starts to feel jealous and demands attention, the three-way bond is broken. Can we delight in the joy that others share?

The perfect three-way bond is in the Trinity. Each person in the Trinity makes room for the others. They stay connected in dynamic joy. This bond started in eternity as the original community of love that perpetually invites us into loving conversation. Moments of pain tempt us to stay outside of this life-giving conversation. Immanuel journaling draws us back. Conversing with the Father, Son and Spirit, as well as with fellow sojourners, reunites us.

In the Trinity, Jesus always points to the Father and the Spirit always testifies about Jesus and the Father loves Jesus and entrusted us to His Spirit. This dynamic of trust, sacrifice and honor is the cornerstone of God's character within the mystery of the Trinity. When we rely on the Spirit and live in the Trinitarian way, it makes a real difference in the way we respond to one another. We become family.

Developing a family identity is needed for maturity. We all become important, contributing members. We belong in the group and cannot be replaced by a substitute so we need not be territorial. We can make room for others to join. But many of us grew up being overlooked or belittled rather than accepted. Fearing that we must always make a place for ourselves, our group participation becomes focused on getting something rather than making room for others.

When we practice Immanuel journaling with a trusted group, we start connecting with God and others at the same time. This is a real and delightful way to form a group identity as God's children. As we rhyme thoughts with God, a space is created within us to become attuned with others. When we listen to a journal entry read aloud, we become the third person in the three way bond as we enjoy the bond between the reader and God. When it is our turn to read, others enjoy our mutual-mind with God. We become people whose identity is interpreted through our connection with God and each other. *i*Sight forms our group identity.

Developing a coherent life story

The value of reading our Immanuel journaling entries out loud to others is explained well by Jim and Chris in their booklet, *Share Immanuel*. Interacting with God is the first half of transformation. Telling the Immanuel story is the other half. When our Immanuel time heals our pain, these authors observe, "Our past memory has been completed successfully, but our mind does not understand what happened enough to change the way we view the future. We can correct our minds by telling the story" (Wilder, 2010). Telling our Immanuel stories also changes how our community sees the future when we share our Immanuel journaling.

While most of our relational identity is operated from the right side of the brain, our narrative memory, procedural memory and outlook for the future is hosted in the verbal left-brain. The left-brain needs a story. Stories tell how the world works, how to solve problems and what we can learn from others. Stories form communities and families. Stories change our view of the future by spreading news to others and improving the way we solve similar situations in the future. Remembering the stories of God builds faith. We need to tell the story of what Immanuel did for us.

Regular practice with Immanuel journaling (including reading our entries out loud) makes relational sense of our life experiences. The incompletely processed, painful moments in our lives inhibit us from telling our life stories in a coherent way and developing close relationships. Immanuel journaling processes the misunderstood or misplaced part of our stories in a way that makes sense in light of God's big redemptive story. This is why it is vitally important that we share our Immanuel journaling entries with others and so develop a coherent story with stronger relationships.

Shalom check

We have all heard people tell stories that lowered our joy, failed to bless us, and made us wish they had kept those stories to themselves. In order for us to ensure that our journal entries are ready to read in a group we recommend running a *shalom check* at the end of every journal writing session.

You will recall that shalom is to be the referee in all we do (Colossians 3:15). Shalom is a sense we get when everything is in the right relationship, at the right time, in the right place, at the right strength and in the right amount for God and people. Shalom tells us we have a mutual-mind with God and see things rightly. Shalom is possible when we have *i*Sight as we hear in Paul's words to the church, "May the Lord of all shalom give you shalom at all times, in all ways and in every place. The Lord continues being with you all" (2 Thessalonians 3:15-16; we have used the word shalom instead of peace).

Our spirit is made for truth, but our brain also seeks shalom. As long as things do not "fit," our mind remains unstable and open to change. When everything makes sense, the right hemisphere closes the door to changing our mind because now we "know." We look for shalom at the end of Immanuel journaling about painful topics. Shalom signals that we have processed painful material all the way through the pain processing pathway. Can we be wrong? Of course! However, when there is no shalom we can be sure we are wrong, that our processing is incomplete. We need to ask God why we do not have shalom and finish the journaling. Sometimes we will need a mature person to attune to us as well until we find shalom.

Since most of us are completely accustomed to living lives without shalom, we come to think of it as normal. In fact, our talkative left hemisphere may not even stop to check whether we have shalom or not. It is important to ask the question aloud. We might have shalom and have never noticed, or we might not have shalom and haven't finished processing a painful experience. In Immanuel journaling, we do not want to read our journals in a group when they are not yet shalom stories.

What does Shalom look like for Immanuel journaling?
- My sense of interacting with God right now is not inhibited. I am able to perceive that God is right here with me and actively working for me.
- My confidence in God is secure and strong. I am confident that reading aloud my Immanuel journaling entry to the community will not hamper my connection with God.
- My weaknesses are shown accurately. I do not need to act stronger than I am or hide my weakness from God or others for fear of loss.
- My sense of peace and Jesus' interactive presence are still there when I reread my journal entry.
- The Immanuel journaling process increased my sense of joy, peace and hope.
- My desire to serve and love others has increased.

We have observed that shalom is amplified as we share stories. The brain is a natural emotional amplifier, and as communities we amplify each other's feelings. When our RCs are off, we amplify problems instead. So when a group is in shalom and someone reads a shalom story, the group will amplify shalom. If people lose shalom when a story is read, we should ask God why the Referee has just blown the "no shalom" whistle. Going through a shalom checklist regularly can be very helpful.

Shalom checklist

- Do I feel peacefully calm? (This topic "fits" together correctly now.)
- Am I sensing God's loving presence?
- Am I confident that nothing can take me away from God's love?
- Am I portraying my weakness accurately?
- Am I still sensing God's interactive presence in my painful memory?
- Have my joy, peace and hope increased?
- Has my desire to love and serve others increased?

If we answered "yes" to these questions, it is safe to assume that we are experiencing shalom. One simple question sums up the list above; "When I think of Jesus in this moment do I feel an authentic sense of His love for me and a growing desire to love others?"

On my own and in my church

Immanuel journaling helps us join the community of love within the body of Christ. Sharing our hearts via Immanuel journaling may seem insignificant, but when done in love it brings abundant life to participants. Sometimes the effects are quickly obvious, and other times the fruit is cumulative.

If Christians brimmed with love and peace, our churches would be overflowing! We imagine an Immanuel presence in small groups, conversations, committee meetings, team meetings and sermons, and as a culture in church that amplifies joy and peace. The beauty of Immanuel journaling is that it helps us become aware of God's presence during painful as well as joyful moments. Additionally, since this interaction is written out we can easily read aloud what we've already written. By sharing our hearts and minds, we participate in a very powerful and unique way in the body of Christ. A tremendous amount of healing is available for anyone willing to engage regularly in Immanuel journaling.

We hope your church will be inspired to run a short three week to three month test. We believe that the results will speak to you as they did to us. Test Immanuel journaling and share your experience with others and with us.

Facilitator's notes

Here are some notes and guidelines to help your group through the Immanuel journaling process. We have found 90 minutes to be a good amount of time for a small group of five to seven people. Feel free to tailor the time allotments to meet your needs. Experiment with your group to find the right flow.

The group can choose to alternate leaders or have someone lead for the month. The first few times, the group can choose to have the facilitator verbally guide the group through the process until it becomes a natural flow for the group. If new people join the group, the chosen facilitator can give the big picture and explain the process of the meeting.

The facilitator can gently let people know they can proceed to the next section. Finding a gentle way to keep time and help the group move forward without interrupting too much is an art we can all develop as facilitators. One suggestion is to let the group know when half the suggested time has passed. Five minutes into the gratitude portion one might say, "This might be a good time to start writing down what you sense God might be saying to you."

Group guidelines and intentions

Each person should be given the group guidelines before the group gathers together.

1. We gather together to listen to God speak to us individually and as a body.
2. We will protect one another in love.
   a. We will create safety in a group by treating each other's weaknesses tenderly.
   b. Whatever is shared in the group stays in the group. If you desire to share a portion of others' interaction with God, ask for their permission.
   c. We commit to keeping our RCs on throughout our time together and honestly ask for help when our RCs have turned off.
   d. We will commit to running the shalom check before we read our Immanuel journaling entries.
3. If anyone wants to share their personal entry outside of the group they have that freedom.

Gathering in the presence of God (10-15 minutes)

Welcome: Welcome people as they arrive. Build joy. Make it clear you are glad to be together in your own way and style.

Check in: Once everyone has arrived and the group is ready to begin, conduct a brief check-in. Fit your check-in to your group. This step is simple and important as it warms up the group and encourages everyone to share something. As people share, be prayerfully attentive. Some suggestions include:
- Each person shares how you are doing on a scale of 1-10. 1 is terrible. 10 is fantastic.
- State in one to three sentences how you are doing.
- Share an image that depicts how you are doing right now.

Opening prayer and intention: We slow ourselves down to open our hearts up to the indwelling presence of Christ. We desire to hear Immanuel speak to us as we share where we are today. We will listen to God and to one another. The facilitator can state the intention aloud each time, or members can take turns reading the prayer.

Prayer Example
> Let us close our eyes and slow our breathing down so that we make ourselves fully available to the loving presence of God. Remember that this breath is the gift of life given to us by our Heavenly Father. Taking a deep breath reminds us that Jesus is closer to us than the air that we breathe. He is closer to us than we are to ourselves. We slow ourselves down and pay attention to our breathing as a way of offering our bodies as a living sacrifice. Spirit of the living God, we are your servants; please speak to us. In Jesus' name we pray. Amen.

Individually interacting with God (35-45 minutes)
Let the group know that we are entering into our own time to interact with God through interactive gratitude and thought-rhyming.

1. **Interactive gratitude (10 minutes)** Still yourself, then start writing to God what you are grateful for right now. (The facilitator reminds participants that it is beneficial if they pay attention to giving thanks for relational aspects of life, and that any sort of gratitude is a fine way to start.)

Example of facilitator's encouragement:
Some of you might be having a hard time finding something you are grateful for this morning. Do not let the exercise of interactive gratitude be a barrier. Start where you are, and share your thoughts with God. You might write in your journal something like, "Father, I am here but still upset about this morning with my family. Can you help me be present with You here and now?"

2. **Thought rhyming (25 - 35 minutes)** Once we are done with interactive gratitude, we can take a moment to ask God a question before we proceed to the next section of the exercise. "Jesus, what do You want to talk about today?" Once we discern the focus of this next conversation, we can begin to write down our impressions from Immanuel. If nothing specific comes up, we can begin with where we are at that present moment, humbly attempting to see life from God's eyes as we wait for His presence. We can then follow the sequence of thought rhyming as listed below.

- I can see you
- I can hear you
- I understand how big of a deal this is for you
- I'm glad to be with you
- I can do something about this with you or for you

Reading aloud (30-40 minutes)
Let the group know that we are entering into our time to read aloud.

1. **Facilitator check:** The facilitator gently gathers people by saying something like this.

Example
How is everyone doing? Maybe we can read in a few minutes. Is everyone ready to read? Let's pause and ask God to guide us; "Spirit, speak to us as a group as we listen to You through one another's stories."

2. **The facilitator reminds the group of the intention and guidelines as we read out loud our entry.**

Example
Let us remember that we are listening to a sacred moment between the Father and His child. Let us take a moment to slow down and run a sha-

lom check in our mind before we begin reading aloud. I encourage each
one of us to turn towards the person reading his or her entry. As that
person shares, let us hold the person in the presence of the Father. After
each person shares, we will pause with a moment of prayerful silence (30
seconds or more as the group is comfortable), imagining the Father being
with that person in a loving and kind way.

3. **Facilitator begins the process of reading and listening by asking, "Who
would like to share first?"** After the first person shares, remember to pause
in prayerful silence. Then the facilitator can say, "Thank you for sharing. Is
there anything that you noticed during the silence?" Give time for the person
to respond since it is not uncommon for someone to hear God in a fresh way
after reading his or her entry.

After the first person shares, the facilitator can suggest going around the
circle. You can also ask, "Who would like to go next?"

4. **Facilitator closes the group time.** The facilitator or another person can
close in prayer. Remind the group to build joy and create belonging as the
group closes. Find your unique ways of creating belonging as you depart the
group. Also, gently share how you are practicing Immanuel journaling outside of the group and encourage one another to do the same.

Example

I'm so glad to be with you and look forward to next week. Last week
when I noticed that my shalom was gone, I found time to interact with
God and called Susan to read my entry. It was so helpful. We do not need
to wait until the next meeting since Jesus is available 24/7 and accessible
to you. Let us also be available for one another throughout the week.

Adding a community shalom check

It is an enriching experience to share aloud about our personal shalom
check in a small group.

"This does give me shalom," or "I am not experiencing shalom at this
point. Maybe I should go back and interact with Jesus some more about this."
However, we can go even further when we develop ways to have a group-wide
shalom check. One important aspect to the community support is taking a
moment to do a shalom check together. The purpose is to grow our trust in
the goodness of God. We pause and ask together, "Does what I have written
give me shalom?" or "Does what you have heard give you shalom?"

The group facilitator is called upon for wisdom and gentleness here. For the most part, if the group is safe and everyone is following basic group guidelines, this part of the process will flow beautifully. If someone isn't experiencing shalom, he or she can gently be encouraged to go back and interact with Jesus. The emphasis is on responding with gentleness to each person and doing our own shalom checks.

If someone is reluctant to share out loud the answer to the question "Does this give you shalom?" it is likely they do not have true shalom. This is a natural part of the process. Gently encourage people to continue their interaction with Immanuel. If there is enough time, you can continue on the spot. If not, encourage the person to find time in the near future to continue interacting with Immanuel.

A concluding word of encouragement

We believe that you will experience the transformation of Christ dwelling within you, speaking to you, revealing how He sees you and sheltering you in tender compassion through Immanuel journaling. This simple tool has enabled us to live with Christ in moments of deep pain and true joy. We have shared fresh life in Christ (koinonia) in more abundant ways. It is our hope and prayer that you test the results of practicing Immanuel journaling. If you see the fruit of the Spirit growing naturally from your Immanuel times, share this practice with others. Let the good news of Jesus Christ become contagious.

Our blessing

May we know the Father's heart and see the Son's compassionate bond with us revealed by the Spirit's power in our hearts. May the Spirit enliven us to seek first the kingdom of God with a growing confidence that the Father will always provide everything we need as we love and serve those near to us.

May the beautiful presence of Immanuel shine light into your heart so that you are free to love as Jesus loves you. May Christ and you love each person in your path and your day. May your life flourish.

Chapter Seven

Frequently Asked Questions (FAQ)

1. How often and when should I practice interactive gratitude or thought rhyming?

It is beneficial to practice the three elements of Immanuel journaling as much as needed. The three elements are 1) interactive gratitude, 2) thought rhyming and 3) reading aloud. With that said, we would like to differentiate between the interactive gratitude and thought rhyming steps of Immanuel journaling. We have noticed that most people are drawn to thought rhyming when they are experiencing pain or going through a difficult period in life. Thought rhyming almost immediately alleviates pain and gives sufferers a sense of hope. It can be more challenging to stay motivated to journal during times of relative comfort. We recommend being in a safe group that meets weekly to practice the full

Immanuel journaling sequence together as a way of maintaining motivation when we are not in pain. Hearing God with great ease is one benefit of regularly conversing with God about the current events in our lives.

We recommend practicing interactive gratitude daily. Interactive gratitude is easier to practice and can be done in shorter periods of time (5 to 10 minutes). This is in contrast to the thought rhyming process that requires more focus and time (25 to 35 minutes). Interactive gratitude builds joy. The daily habit of interactive gratitude increases our awareness of God's Immanuel presence and His goodness towards us. Moreover, the regular practice of interactive gratitude will allow our conversation with God to deepen more quickly.

Those who have been practicing interactive gratitude and thought rhyming regularly report that even when using interactive gratitude alone, they notice God's response resembles the thought rhyming sequence. During God's response to our thanksgiving, we notice that God reveals areas of our lives we might overlook as unimportant. God does not wait until our pain becomes unbearable but initiates restoration whenever we converse with Him.

2. What if I don't know what to write about, feel resistant or cannot feel grateful?

We recommend starting where we are at the present moment. If we don't know what to write about, we can tell God honestly and state that we are feeling blank, resistant, angry, hungry or whatever we are experiencing at the moment. We encourage becoming aware of what our physical bodies are feeling right now. Body awareness will help restore our RCs. When we recognize our resistance and allow God to talk with us *while we feel resistant*, it becomes much easier to move through the resistance. We have noticed that gratitude emerges as a byproduct of being accepted by God, no matter what state we are in when we come to Him.

3. Is a shalom check necessary?

Yes, a shalom check is necessary and beneficial. A shalom check allows people to check what they are hearing against the character of God as revealed in scripture. A shalom check tests for the witness of the Spirit within us and between us. A shalom check reveals if we can accept what we have written as truth about ourselves. Our mutual-mind states with God are always subject to distortion from our side. When we are just learning to rhyme thoughts with God we will "hear" things that sound pious, religious, righteous, condemning, accusatory, demeaning and frightening. Assuming that we have heard God correctly would be a MAJOR mistake. In fact, we should never reach the point where we assume we are hearing God without distortions. However, as Colossians 3:15 and other scriptures point out, there is a peace that goes beyond our understanding that tells us what we are thinking is true and good in a way that settles deeply into our hearts and souls. We are so accustomed to living without this shalom peace that we forget to check whether it is there, particularly when we are working on thought rhyming with God, we should never fail to check for shalom. To fail to check for shalom is to risk deception.

The shalom check may be introduced differently, depending on the setting. We want to create a space where this can be done gently. At the same time, everyone is responsible for running a shalom check of their own at all times.

a.   Peer settings: In this setting we assume that a few close friends who trust each other get together to practice Immanuel journaling. We recommend everyone become familiar with the group guidelines and intentions. Having read and understood the guidelines, we suggest that members take responsibility for being mindful of their own RCs and shalom check. Give participants permission to speak when they feel uneasy. Gentle shalom checking is a safeguard for the individual as well as the group.

b.   Church settings: In this setting, we are assuming that there is a facilitator who has more experience in Immanuel journaling taking the leadership role. Having a leader allows for a more diverse group of people who might be in different stages of life. Moreover, there might be less connections within the group; therefore, the intentional shalom check becomes even more essential.

The group facilitator provides wisdom and gentleness here. For the most part, if the group is safe and everyone is following basic group safety guidelines, this part of the process will flow beautifully. If we (as a facilitator/leader) perceived that a member misunderstood God or did not pass the shalom check, the person can gently be encouraged to go back and interact with Jesus. The emphasis is on responding with gentleness to each person and doing our own shalom checks.

4. Can I use "interactive gratitude" to create a new sense of normal?

Yes, interactive gratitude can give us a new normal. Do we wake up feeling anxious? Do pleasant experiences drift away quickly? Our brain works hard to keep things "normal." Our sense of normal is set before we are two years old according to how things generally feel in our lives at that time. If our family is depressed from a death or illness, our parents are anxious due to lack of money or war, or if their personalities tend to be angry – all these factors contribute to our sense of normal. At about the age we are learning to talk, our brain sets these environmental feelings as the "normal" for our lives.

Later in life we may struggle against an angry, worried, depressed or un-loved sense of normal, but our brain quickly finds its way back to miser-able each morning or after something positive happens. We believe that good things don't last and that miserable is normal every day. Without retraining our brain to a new normal, that is exactly what will happen.

1. The first step to a new normal is learning to feel appreciation in my body. Appreciation, interactive gratitude and thankfulness will all work provided I notice what I feel like in my body during the emo-tions. Noticing the body sensations insures that the right parts of my brain are working together (prefrontal cortex, anterior cingulate and insula). When my brain discovers that I can feel appreciation at will, a new range of possibilities opens for me. I can open this door through interactive gratitude (Chapter 3).

2. The second step toward a new normal is learning to sustain the feeling of appreciation until I can feel appreciation for five straight minutes. To do this, I use the interactive gratitude exercise to collect a series of appreciation experiences and memories by giving them names like island sunrise, morning coffee, Fido at lake, Julie's birth-day. Now I can keep my appreciation going longer by remembering one appreciation experience after another. When I can do this for five minutes, my brain realizes that I can feel this as long as I like.

3. The third step to a new normal comes by practicing five minutes of interactive gratitude three times a day for a month. Starting and ending my day with appreciation and throwing in a dose in the middle helps my brain realize, "I can do this all day." The marvel of our brain as a learning machine is that once it knows how to feel good, it can keep that good feeling going and have a good feeling any time of the day. It decides, "I'll make this my new normal!"

5. What is the difference between the three types of the Immanuel process 1) Immanuel journaling, 2) Facilitated Immanuel process for an individual and 3) Group Immanuel?

Characteristics	Immanuel Journaling	Facilitated Individual	Group Immanuel
Learning time for mature leaders (to lead others)	1-2 hours	6-12 hours	5-8 hours
Learning time for mature people (to lead others)	1-2 hours	18 hours	12 hours
Learning time for immature people (to use effectively)	1-5 hours	40+ hours	Not recommended
Use for disasters	Varies by situation	Requires most training and facilitators	Most useful
Use for secret traumas	Best for building community	Most useful when relational failure in the community is a major source of trauma	Most useful method when trust is low between people
Ability to resolve deep issues	High	High	High
Ease of problem solving with blockages	Slow but most structured	Best for resolving blockages	Cannot resolve
Difficulties	• Requires literacy • Best in individual-istic cultures	• Facilitator confi-dence is required • Most susceptible to human intru-sion	• Inability to feel appreciation • Very susceptible to environmental noise
Time required	20 min. but open ended	10-30 min. but open ended	10-15 min.
People helped simultaneously	Limited to room need to write in a quiet room	One	Hundreds
Develops joy	Best	Once the method is mastered	Least
Youngest age to use	8-13 years old (assisted)	2 years old	4-6 years old (with care)

Immanuel journaling is the most structured of the Immanuel methods and simplest to use, learn or direct. The structure allows people with little training and maturity to learn interactive gratitude, thought rhyming and community sharing. This method is the most simple to teach during short visits to other countries provided the group is literate and allows individual expression. It is not well suited to places with oral or group cultures or where written evidence endangers believers.

Comparing methods between the three types of the Immanuel process 1) Immanuel journaling, 2) Facilitated Immanuel process for an individual and 3) Group Immanuel

Immanuel Journaling	Facilitated Individual	Group Immanuel

Interactive gratitude
• Thank you
  » Our gratitude to God
  » God's response
 	
Thought rhyming
• I see you
• I hear you
• I understand you
• I am glad to be with you
• I give you
 	
Reading journal aloud
• Read aloud
• Check for shalom
• Read aloud in group (option)
• Check for shalom (in group)
• Tell shalom story
	• Find three named appreciation memories
	• Ask God to help pick you pick one
	• 2 min. of appreciation
	• Check for God's presence
	• Ask God the question "What does God want you to know about…"
	• Count to 15
	• Check for shalom
	  » No – return to question
	  » Yes – continue
	• Ask what changed
	• Tell shalom story
		• Ask God for help
		• Find appreciation memory
		• *No appreciation - Return to start*
		• Check for God's presence
		• 2 min. of appreciation
		• *No appreciation - Return to start*
		• Ask group question for God, "What does God want you to know about…"
		• Check appreciation every 90 seconds for duration (2-3 times)
		• Check for shalom
		• Leave unfinished business with God for later
		• Ask what changed
		• Tell shalom story to neighbor

Group Immanuel is best for reaching large groups, whether the traumas are from private or publicly known causes, but the fabric of the society is supportive. Group Immanuel is easily learned by mature leaders regardless of culture or education. This method works very well in group and oral tradition cultures. The process has few side effects but does not resolve blockages for individuals who have them.

Facilitated Individual Immanuel is most similar to traditional therapies and prayer ministry. While the procedure is much simpler and safer than methods requiring counselor training, some healing, maturity and confidence is needed to lead the process. The process is best done in groups of three with a facilitator and prayer-observer working together.

All three methods have the same objective – helping people learn to remove the blockages to interaction with God. All three are used for building joy and relationship with God. All three are used for resolving hurts. All three are useful for building community, receiving guidance and propagating recovery.

6. Can people abuse Immanuel journaling by claiming their thoughts and feelings are from God?

The basic purpose of Immanuel journaling focuses on developing a mind that mirrors how God thinks about the daily business of our lives. To want to elevate anything from Immanuel journaling to the status of "God said" is already an abuse. A better phrase might be, "I am feeling more peaceful now since I am able to see the situation (or person) the way God sees than before I journaled." However, the problem with this peace is that it could possibly be from our tendency to justify ourselves (narcissism) to give us a sense of liking what we want to justify.

It is possible to create shalom in two ways: 1) I synchronize with what God is doing through *i*Sight. Others who are also synchronized with Immanuel will feel and amplify shalom and it will produce a tender response to weakness. 2) I synchronize everything to myself (narcissism) so I feel shalom, but it does not bring peace to others who are using *i*Sight and produces self-justification rather than tenderness towards others.

7. Are there any hazards associated with Immanuel journaling?

While the process of Immanuel journaling is not associated with many hazards from its use, there is always the risk factor of spiritual abuse when communities are not tender toward the weakness in others. If reading one's journal in community is greeted in ways that lower joy levels, participants may be hurt – not by the journaling but by the community response. Similar damage is done when journaling is read as spiritual justification for one's own iniquities.

There are three quite harmful and deviant practices that sometimes develop in communities who use the Immanuel process:

1. Using the Immanuel process to see what God thinks about someone else is dangerous. While we have God's promise that He will clean things that block our hearts from Him, there is no similar promise that God will tell us what is in anyone else's heart.

2. Using the Immanuel process to hear God for someone else is dangerous. It may be tempting to ask someone who seems to hear God more clearly than we do what God has to say to us. The long-term results of relying on this practice to hear from God are all bad.

3. Using the Immanuel process to "test reality" of such things as memories or events is dangerous. We have no promises from God that He will reveal accurate accounts of history to us on request. Attempts to find out "what really happened" through Immanuel are totally unreliable – that is not what the process does.

When forming Immanuel journaling groups we recommend at least three or more people participate in the group at a given time. We desire to promote a group identity through three-way bonds instead of encouraging two-way bonds except when it is used for couples.

8. What is the role of the Bible as the written word of God in increasing our ability to listen to God's voice?

We believe that God speaks to us in many ways, the Bible being the main and most reliable source. While interactive gratitude and thought-rhyming are more indirect ways of listening to God, we find that they are very helpful. The main reason we encourage people to enter into a conversation with God beyond traditional Bible study is that people sometimes stop interacting with God when we feel that listening to God can only come from extensive Bible study.

However, we want to emphasize the importance and necessity of engaging ourselves in studying the Bible on a regular basis in order for us to increase our ability to recognize God's voice. We believe that getting to know God and His character (who God says He is) is a crucial part of increasing our ability to recognize God's voice.

9. Isn't Immanuel journaling "putting words in God's mouth?" I learned that God can only speak through the Bible. Can I write down Bible verses as God's responses?

In Immanuel journaling we can only be sure that we are writing our thoughts. The closer these thoughts come to God's thoughts, the more shalom exists. From Satan's temptation of Jesus (Matt 4:1ff), we learn that not even quoting scripture will guarantee us God's thoughts. When we read scripture we also see its meaning through the thick glasses of what those words mean to us. If we limit what God can say to us through scripture, then God can never lead us to Boston (as an example) as Boston is not in any Bible texts.

If you grew up in a church where you were taught that God would only speak through the Bible, it can be very challenging for you to venture into writing down your impression of God outside of what the Bible says exactly. In this case feel free to write down the Bible verses as God's response to you. Afterwards, run a simple test by asking yourself, "Does this sound and feel like Jesus is right here next to me, speaking to me?" If your answer is "Yes," then great. If your answer is "No" or "I am not sure," read the verses aloud to yourself. Is Jesus right next to you personally speaking the Bible verses as God's tender and caring response to you? Afterwards, personalize and write the verses in a conversational way. See if this gives you a sense that God personally spoke to you.

The value of writing down God's written words in a conversational and personal way is to increase our attachment with God. Remember that the Level 1 brain always monitors whether or not something (or God) is personally meaningful to us.

10. What are other resources for Immanuel journaling?

See Resources page for more.

References

Lehman, K. (2011). *Outsmarting Yourself*, 52-282.

Wilder, E. J. (2004). *Living With Men*, 36-45.

Wilder, E.J. & Coursey, C. M. (2010). *Share Immanuel*, 5.

Wilder, E. J., Khouri, E., Coursey, C. M., & Sutton, S. (2013). *Joy Starts Here*, 44-47.

Glossary of Terms

Appreciation - Recognizing the value of someone or something. As followers of Christ we recognize all good things are gifts from God.

Attuned interaction - The sense that someone "gets us" and we are accurately understood. We trust that someone understands us sensitively, tenderly and accurately.

Control center - The brain's right hemisphere holds an emotional regulation structure called the control center. This four-level control center tops the command hierarchy of every brain. Identity, *who I am*, resides at the top (Level 4) of the control center in an area called the prefrontal cortex. Below *who I am*, the cingulate cortex at Level 3, synchronizes life rhythms. The lower two levels control basic evaluations (Level 2) and personal reality (Level 1). The primary development of the control center is in the first two years of life, is primarily nonverbal, and depends on proper stimulation of the brain.

Group identity - While not well recognized in the Western world where independence is highly valued, we become part of a people as infants who are learning to relate and speak. During our young adult years, we form a peer group identity that is further identified with our styles, values and lifestyle. During our young adult life, the brain is rewired so that the survival of our group becomes more important than our individual survival. We are also wired to think and feel many things in common with our group identity without being conscious of where this influence arises.

Immanuel - The name given to Jesus meaning God with us. Highlighted because Jesus is the clearest picture of who God truly is.

Immanuel Journaling - The process of writing down what we are grateful to God for and then moving into a process of sensing and listening to His compassionately attuned response. Finally, we share with safe brothers and sisters in Christ.

Immanuel Lifestyle - A moment by moment intention to live by the indwelling presence of God as our focal point (priority).

Immanuel Process - Dr. Lehman uses this term for a process of trauma resolution that begins with a secure attachment to God and the awareness of His presence.

Interactive gratitude - The process of writing to God what we are grateful for and pausing to write down what we sense God saying to us in response to our appreciation.

*i***Sight** - *i*Sight is having the recognition that God is present, is truly good and perseveres in doing good for us.

Metabolize pain - Experiences of pain need to go through a pain-processing pathway in our brains in order to fully metabolize and heal our wounds.

Mutual-mind states - The structure in the brain called the cingulate cortex makes it possible for meaningful communication to occur between two different minds by establishing a mutual-mind state. When establishing a mutual-mind state, we learn to think and feel the way people we love think and feel.

Pain processing pathway - Pain-processing refers to the normal way painful emotions or experiences are fully resolved in our brains.

Relational joy - The experience of knowing someone is glad to be with us; likewise it is the experience of being glad to be with someone or remembering these moments.

Shalom - Shalom is a state of harmony where everything works together, makes sense and is good. Shalom is the "peace of Christ." Furthermore, Colossians 3:15 tells us that we should let shalom act like a referee in our lives who "stops the action" every time shalom is missing.

Shalom check - A shalom check tests for the witness of the Spirit within us and between us, whether we can accept what we have written as truth about ourselves and if our experience matches God's character as revealed in Scripture.

Synchronize - The process at Level 3 of the brain's control center that allows us to match energy levels, share mutual mind states, amplify joy, and take the time to rest as needed. Internally, our control center synchronizes to work properly and externally, our relationships synchronize to keep us connected. We synchronize with God through Jesus who spoke what He heard His Father speaking, and did what He watched His Father doing. Synchronization brings shalom.

Thought poetry - Poetry in scripture does not rhyme sounds, it follows the Hebrew pattern and rhymes thoughts. This means that as God's poetry; our thoughts can rhyme with our Heavenly Father's.

Thought rhyming - We know that as we become intimate with someone we begin to be able to finish each other's sentences and thoughts. In a deep authentic mutual-mind state, we actually don't know where our thought stops and the others' begins.

Three-way bond - While mutual-mind states can only be shared by two people at a time, our group identity requires three or more people to share an identity. The Life Model calls this family way of bonding a three-way bond.

Immanuel Resources

Share Immanuel
Booklet

Immanuel
Taking Healing to the World
Audio CD

2011
Share Immanuel
Evenings Audio CD

Available at
www.lifemodelworks.org

More Immanuel Resources

To learn more about
Immanuel Training, visit
www.alivewell.org

With the development of Immanuel Prayer Training, Alive & Well has had over 400 students from over 90 different churches attend training events based on the work of Dr. Karl Lehman, Dr. Jim Wilder and Ed Khouri.

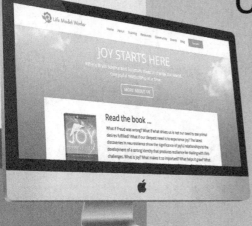

Run the **Life Model Works** curriculum

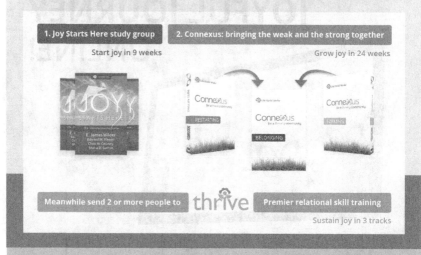

1. Joy Starts Here study group
Start joy in 9 weeks

2. Connexus: bringing the weak and the strong together
Grow joy in 24 weeks

Meanwhile send 2 or more people to thrive   **Premier relational skill training**
Sustain joy in 3 tracks

Attend a **Life Model Works** event

- RoundTable web events
- Thrive Relational Skill Training
- Joy Starts Here city events
- Joy Rekindled Marriage Weekend
- Annual Gathering
- and more...

Visit **lifemodelworks.org/events**
for dates and locations